fresh & herby

fresh & herby

Add flavour and
fragrance to your
favourite recipes

contributing editor:
Joanna Farrow

southwater

This edition is published by Southwater

Southwater is an imprint of Anness Publishing Ltd
Hermes House, 88–89 Blackfriars Road, London SE1 8HA
tel. 020 7401 2077; fax 020 7633 9499
www.southwaterbooks.com; info@anness.com

© Anness Publishing Ltd 2003

This edition distributed in the UK by
The Manning Partnership Ltd
6 The Old Dairy, Melcombe Road
Bath BA2 3LR
tel. 01225 478 444; fax 01225 478 440
sales@manning-partnership.co.uk

This edition distributed in the USA and Canada by
National Book Network
4720 Boston Way
Lanham, MD 20706
tel. 301 459 3366; fax 301 459 1705
www.nbnbooks.com

This edition distributed in Australia by
Pan Macmillan Australia
Level 18, St Martins Tower
31 Market St
Sydney, NSW 2000
tel. 1300 135 113; fax 1300 135 103
customer.service@macmillan.com.au

This edition distributed in New Zealand by
The Five Mile Press (NZ) Ltd
PO Box 33–1071, Takapuna
Unit 11/101–111 Diana Drive
Glenfield, Auckland 10
tel. (09) 444 4144; fax (09) 444 4518
fivemilenz@xtra.co.nz

A CIP catalogue record for this book is available from the
British Library.

Publisher: Joanna Lorenz
Managing Editor: Helen Sudell
Project Editor: Simona Hill
Designer: Nigel Partridge
Production Controller: Ben Worley

Previously published as part of a larger compendium, *Herbs*

10 9 8 7 6 5 4 3 2 1

NOTES

For all recipes, quantities are given in both metric and
imperial measures and, where appropriate, measures are also
given in standard cups and spoons. Follow one set, but not a
mixture because they are not interchangeable.

Standard spoon and cup measures are level.
1 tsp = 5ml, 1 tbsp = 15ml, 1 cup = 250ml/8fl oz

Australian standard tablespoons are 20ml. Australian readers
should use 3 tsp in place of 1 tbsp for measuring small
quantities of gelatine, flour, salt etc.

Medium (US large) eggs are used unless otherwise stated.

ACKNOWLEDGEMENTS

Photographers: Karl Adamson, Edward Allwright, Steve Baxter,
Nicki Dowey, James Duncan, Gus Filgate, John Freeman, Ian
Garlick, Michelle Garrett, Peter Henley, John Heseltine,
Amanda Heywood, Janine Hosegood, Andrea Jones, Dave
Jordan, Dave King, Don Last, William Lingwood, Patrick
McLeavey, Michael Michaels, Steve Moss, Thomas Odulate,
Debbie Patterson, Craig Robertson, Sam Stowell, Polly
Wreford.

Recipes: Catherine Atkinson, Alex Barker, Angela Boggiano,
Ruby Le Bois, Carla Capalbo, Lesley Chamberlain, Kit Chan,
Jaqueline Clark, Maxine Clark, Frances Cleary, Carole
Clements, Andi Clevely, Trish Davies, Roz Denny, Patrizia
Diemling, Stephanie Donaldson, Matthew Drennan, Joanna
Farrow, Rafi Fernandez, Christine France, Silvano Franco,
Sarah Gates, Shirley Gill, Brian Glover, Nicola Graimes,
Rosamund Grant, Juliet Harbutt, Jessica Houdret, Deh-Ta
Hsiung, Shehzad Hussain, Christine Ingram, Judy Jackson,
Peter Jordan, Manisha Kanini, Soheila Kimberley, Lucy Knox,
Masaki Ko, Sara Lewis, Patricia Lousada, Gilly Love, Norma
MacMillan, Sue Maggs, Sally Mansfield, Maggie Mayhew,
Norma Miller, Sallie Morris, Janice Murfitt, Annie Nichols,
Elizabeth Lambert Oritz, Katherine Richmond, Anne Sheasby,
Jenni Shapter, Liz Trigg, Hilaire Walden, Laura Washburn,
Stuart Walton, Steven Wheeler, Kate Whiteman, Elizabeth
Wolf-Cohen, Jenni Wright.

Stylists: Alison Austin, Shannon Beare, Madeleine Brehaut,
Frances Cleary, Tessa Evelegh, Marilyn Forbes, Annabel Ford,
Nicola Fowler, Michelle Garrett, Carole Handslip, Cara
Hobday, Kate Jay, Maria Kelly, Lucy McKelvie, Marion
McLornan, Marion Price, Jane Stevenson, Helen Trent, Sophie
Wheeler, Judy Williams, Elizabeth Wolf-Cohen.

Home Economists: Eliza Baird, Alex Barker, Julie Beresford,
Sascha Brodie, Stephanie England, Annabel Ford, Christine
France, Carole Handslip, Kate Jay, Jill Jones, Clare Lewis,
Sara Lewis, Bridget Sargeson, Joy Skipper, Jenni Shapter,
Carole Tennant.

contents

Introduction	6
Herb Gardens	8
Harvesting, Drying & Storing Herbs	14
Herb Directory	16
Soups, Salads & Appetizers	24
Fish, Poultry & Meat	44
Vegetarian	66
Breads & Bakes	88
Desserts, Ices & Sorbets	106
Index	128

INTRODUCTION

Herbs are plants we associate with natural healing, fragrant aromas, essential oils and appetizing food. Although they have been used with confidence for thousands of years, scientists are still discovering just how valuable herbs are in the prevention and cure of many illnesses.

Centuries ago herbs were revered for their spiritual and religious associations and were only latterly used in the kitchen. In the East, gardens were planted with herbs as a peaceful retreat for meditation and thought. This idea gradually spread to Western monasteries, and the discovery of new and exotic species led to experimentation with herbs as a

Below: Herbs are not always used as a delicate flavouring, they can also be the main ingredient of a dish.

cure-all. Feverfew, as the name suggests, was used to alleviate colds and fevers. Hyssop was used in biblical times as a cleanser and antiseptic, mint as a digestive aid and chamomile as a sedative. Almost every illness could be treated with one or more of the ever-widening array of herbs.

Established and newly discovered herbs were planted out in regular, formal plots so that doctors, scientists and botanists could study and experiment with them. These physic gardens led to the trend for formal herb gardens, much loved by wealthy landowners, particularly during the Middle Ages. Often walled, laid out in meticulously designed patterns of colour, size and type, and divided by small footpaths, they were a mark of affluence and social status. Today, many physic gardens have been

Above: Garlic and rosemary are instantly recognizable by their delicious taste and splendid aromas.

re-created and there are splendid herb gardens that we can visit, giving us the opportunity to appreciate the wide variety of herbs available.

As we seek a healthier lifestyle, we look to natural remedies to provide a gentle, alternative approach to curing diseases. As a result there is a great deal of research into the medicinal powers of herbs. However, it is our appreciation of good food and our love of gardens and gardening that has kept our fascination for herbs alive. Herbs are simply stunning: a mass of their delicate flowers, ranging from the softest white through to vibrant lavender can be an absolute treat for the eyes. Better still is the wonderful fragrance they exude as you brush past them on a warm summer's evening when their volatile oils perfume the air.

Herbs have one great advantage over so many other plants: they can be grown almost anywhere in any quantity, so space is never a problem. A few pots of basic culinary herbs in a sunny spot near the kitchen door can provide a substantial supply for the kitchen. With a little more space, herb borders or small islands of herbs randomly planted and growing into one another provide a

highly desirable, yet slightly unkempt-looking cottage-garden effect. On a grander scale there are the manicured, formal gardens that need plenty of room and attention to keep them looking good. Here, a vast selection of different herbs can be grown alongside each other, even if there are relatively few that will be used regularly.

In cooking, herbs add a feast of natural flavour that enhances almost every food, whether sweet or savoury. Combinations like lamb with rosemary, potatoes in mint butter, salmon with dill, and tomatoes with basil have become classics that we simply cannot improve upon. Due to the impact of their flavours, herbs can turn the simplest dish into the freshest, liveliest treat. Two or three complimentary herbs, chopped and added to garlic butter and melted over grilled chicken or fish or freshly steamed vegetables, transform a dish into something special, equally as good as any complicated sauce. Aromatic herbs like parsley, coriander (cilantro), mint, chives and basil can be whisked into a salad dressing or simply sprinkled over salad leaves, totally transforming the appearance and flavour. Even sweet dishes benefit from the herb treatment.

Below: Lavender can be used in both sweet and savoury dishes, where its soft floral scent imparts a delicate flavour.

Infusing cream with tarragon, bay, rosemary or mint before making ice cream and other creamy desserts can only enhance its overall flavour. Finally, herbs are traditionally used for flavouring drinks. Herbal teas are the most obvious choice; steeping sprigs of lemon balm, mint or chamomile in hot water produces various therapeutic qualities as well as making a refreshing drink. More popular now are chilled juices and smoothies that combine fresh fruits and vegetables in healthy drinks with herbs such as basil, mint, fennel, parsley and lemon balm.

How the cook sources herbs is a question of personal preference. For many there is no better way than to grow herbs from seeds or small plants, nurturing them through the spring to provide an abundance of supplies that last right through to the winter. For others the supermarkets are the best source. If you do have a large herb garden you will have more than enough for culinary use even if you are constantly out there picking and

Above: Herbs can make an otherwise bland dish a flavourful success. Here pretty flowers also add visual appeal.

pruning. If this is the case, you could make decorative use of herbs around the house. A summer dining table looks absolutely stunning decorated with little posies of fresh herbs tucked into vases. Some are best picked at the last minute, but others like borage, chives, lemon geranium, rosemary, bay, thyme, oregano and sage might last for days. Enhance the herb posies with a few pale pink or cream roses and the effect is soft and romantic. Later in the season, herbs that have seeded, like parsley, fennel and angelica, also look good in floral arrangements. The decorative attributes of herbs don't end there. Small bundles of almost any dried herbs can be tied with ribbon or string to make posies for the bathroom or bedroom, their wonderful scents perfuming the room and beyond, or why not use herbs in the traditional way to scent a bath or to freshen linen?

HERB GARDENS

Whatever the size and site of your garden, if you love cooking you will always be able to find a small corner of the garden near the kitchen in which to grow a ready supply of favourite herbs for use in the cooking pot.

PLANNING A HERB GARDEN

Before planting out, it's worth spending a little time planning the herb garden. There are no fixed rules as to what to start with and how much to grow. As with any gardening there is a certain amount of trial and error. Not every herb will grow well in every garden and it may well take a couple of seasons to determine which grow most successfully. You will also need to consider the type of garden you want

Below: Formal herb gardens contained within clipped borders require careful planning and cultivation.

to develop. A formal garden that uses plants as edging takes a few years to mature whereas a brick or gravel-surrounded bed will look pretty within a season, and herbs grown in containers look effective within weeks. There is no correct time of year to start the garden, although planting the herbs out in the spring allows plenty of time for them to develop.

Many herbs such as rosemary, marjoram, oregano, sage and thyme enjoy maximum sunshine, while others, like mint, chervil and chives, prefer partial shade. Generally they all need protection from the wind and this can be provided by low hedges, walls, fences and taller bushes and shrubs. Most herbs prefer a well-drained soil,

Right: Herb gardens cultivated for culinary use can be laid out in an attractive, colourful and formal design.

particularly those of Mediterranean origin. To lighten a heavy clay soil, work in some sand and/or grit from a garden centre (not builder's sand) before planting out.

Below: A clipped bay surrounded by colourful lavender makes a glorious, scented centrepiece for this garden. Both plants have many uses in the kitchen.

Leafy herbs grown solely for culinary use can be successfully grown in surprisingly little space, such as a small bed, container, hanging basket or, if space is really at a premium, indoors on a window sill. Alternatively, grow them in amongst other border plants.

Remember that accessibility is very important. You do not want to go traipsing through wet grass or soil to gather herbs for cooking, so plant them in the most convenient spot nearest to the kitchen. The more common, most frequently used herbs can be planted near the front of the plot while those rarely used can flourish in a more out-of-the-way spot. Stepping stones and small brick or gravel paths can be laid so that you can easily get to less accessible herbs.

Annual herbs like chervil, coriander (cilantro), basil and dill will die down at the end of the season and need replanting the following spring. It is worth distributing these amongst perennial herbs like chives, marjoram, oregano, sage, thyme, rosemary, fennel and parsley, which start to thrive very early in the spring following mild winters.

Some herbs like mint, borage and chives have a tendency to spread

Above: Herbs planted in-between paving stones and along paths make good use of limited space.

vigorously. These are best planted in separate containers so they don't monopolize the whole plot. If you want to grow mint with the other herbs, use a bucket with holes in the base and submerge it in the plot as a way of containing the mint's growth. Do not be tempted to grow too many different types of herbs to start with. You can always add more the following season.

Herb Borders

When space is limited, a small border or bed of herbs meets most culinary requirements, even if interspersed with other non-herbal plants. If there is simply insufficient space, supplement it with additional tubs or containers on the patio or near the kitchen door.

Plant taller herbs such as lovage, bay, fennel and angelica at the back of the plot with smaller herbs at the front, to create an interesting height graduation. If the plot is wide, disperse stepping stones or bricks into the soil to make the herbs at the back more accessible.

Another idea is to create a graduated rockery which also provides easy access to all the herbs. This looks particularly attractive for sun-loving herbs that thrive in hot climates. Once planted amongst the rocks, the soil can be scattered with scree (small irregular rocks of about 2–5cm/¾–2in).

Above: This herb wheel makes a splendid focal point for a large garden.

Herb Wheels

These were a popular feature in Victorian gardens when large wooden cartwheels were widely available. They provide a great way of containing a small selection of leafy culinary herbs. Before use, the wheel must be treated with a plant-friendly preservative to stop the wood from rotting. It is then set down on the prepared plot so the spaces between the spokes can be filled with different herbs. Simply saw off some of the spokes if they are too close together.

The same idea can be created using bricks. This has the added advantage that the herb garden can be designed to a size that suits the garden space and culinary requirements. The choice of herbs is entirely dependent upon individual preference, but aesthetically a selection of low-growing herbs of similar heights looks very effective around the edges, perhaps with a taller plant in the centre.

Island Beds

Planting herbs in a round or rectangular island bed provides easy access and can be designed to fit any available space. In larger beds lay narrow paths through the plot to separate the different herbs and prevent invasive herbs growing into the others. A wide brick or gravel path makes an attractive, practical surround. As with all herb gardens, plant the taller herbs to create a backdrop against the others. A bay tree makes an impressive focal point in the centre of the bed. Alternatively, use a large and attractive urn or garden pot, planted with a small bay, lavender or rose bush.

Formal Box-edged Garden

This is the most ambitious type of herb garden. You will need at least a 4m/13ft-square area of flat space, and the garden will take several years for the box edging to mature. A simple box-edged garden can be divided into four small beds, separated by two paths which cross over in the centre. The corners of the beds can be cut away in the centre to allow for a large potted centrepiece such as a small bay or lavender bush. Plant the young box plants fairly closely together around the edges of the beds so they grow together for trimming into a tightly clipped "wall".

Raised Herb Bed

These are ideal for small gardens where there is little or no planting area, such as in a small courtyard, or where the soil is unsuitable. This is often the case with gardens on heavy clay that many herbs dislike. A raised herb bed can be built to any shape or size in timber or stone, or, more formally, using a brickwork frame. Raised garden beds can also make gardening easier for the

disabled or elderly, as the planting, tending and gathering becomes so much more manageable and easily contained. The height of a raised bed is a matter of personal preference; they can be any height from about 30–45cm/12–18in.

Timber Beds

These can be built to any height, and composed of flat planks or narrow, halved tree trunks, secured into box shapes at the corners. Before using any timber, treat with a wood preservative that is suitable for plants.

Stone Beds

Beds walled with two or three layers of rustic stone look really effective and make a simple way of containing herbs in a small or narrow bed.

Brick Beds

These are both durable and attractive, particularly if made using old bricks. Check they are frostproof as ordinary house bricks might not be suitable. Thoroughly consider the site, shape and size of the bed before starting work. They can be laid out as functional squares or rectangles, in decorative shapes, or made to fit a corner of the garden.

Left: This island bed has paths through the centre to ensure easy access to all the herbs.

MAKING A RAISED BED

Raised beds can be laid out as functional squares and rectangles or made to fit a corner of the garden.

YOU WILL NEED
   dowel, string, fine sand and builder's set square
   concrete made of one part cement to four parts ballast
   bricks
   mortar made of one part cement to four parts of sharp or builder's sand
   waterproof paint
   rubble
   gravel or pea shingle (pea stone)
   topsoil
   potting compost (soil mix)

1 Mark out the shape of the bed on the ground, using dowel and string. Use a builder's set square to mark the right angles. Define the lines with a dribble of fine sand.

2 Dig out the soil along the markings to a depth and width of 15cm/6in. Fill in with concrete to within 5cm/2in of the top. Firm down, level and leave for 24 hours to set.

3 Build up four or five courses of bricks and set into mortar, checking frequently with a spirit level.

4 Tidy up the mortar around the edges while still wet, using a pointing trowel. Leave to harden.

5 Coat the inside wall with waterproof paint. Put in a layer of rubble, then gravel or pea shingle for drainage.

6 Fill in with topsoil and add a top layer of a potting compost. Plant up the bed with your chosen herbs.

GROWING LEAFY HERBS IN CONTAINERS

Most herbs grow very well in containers, and there is a wide variety to choose from. A collection of several containers of different materials and shapes makes an attractive display on the patio. Do not choose anything too large if you want to be able to move pots around, for example, when you want to bring them into a sheltered position during the winter.

For convenience, several different herbs can be grown in one container, but bear in mind that they are not all compatible. Mint and parsley do not grow well together and fennel does not mix with caraway, dill or coriander (cilantro). Mint, tarragon and chives are best grown in separate containers as they will stifle any other herbs they are mixed with. Some herbs, like rosemary, thyme, marjoram and sage, like a sunny spot, while mint, chervil and chives prefer a more filtered light.

During the spring and summer months all container-grown herbs need daily watering, particularly those grown in very small pots, as they can dry out in a matter of hours. However, do not be tempted to overwater any herbs. The soil should never become waterlogged.

Growing Herbs in Pots

Whatever type of pot you choose make sure there is a hole in the base for drainage. Fill the base with a layer of broken terracotta or stones and then a layer of grit or sand before filling with potting compost (soil mix). Once the herbs have been planted and watered, raise the container off the ground using wooden battens or clay pot supports to free the drainage holes and prevent clogging.

Hanging Baskets

These look lovely filled with a mixture of upright and trailing herbs. Go for sturdy herbs such as sage, thyme, curled parsley and rosemary. Before filling with compost (soil mix), line the basket with moss to stop the compost falling through. Soak the moss and compost well before planting by standing the basket in a large container of water. Avoid hanging the basket in a very exposed area.

Above: Herbs are ideal plants to grow on the kitchen windowsill.

Growing Herbs Indoors

Most culinary herbs will thrive indoors provided they are sited in a light and sunny position and enjoy a fairly humid environment, away from central heating and severe temperature extremes. Indoor herbs benefit from being grown collectively because of the massed humidity.

Indoor herbs are less likely to grow into bushy, thriving plants because they are growing in a less natural environment. One way to overcome this problem is to alternate pots grown on the windowsill with some kept outside. Choose as large a pot as you can to fit the space available. Basil is one of the most successful herbs to grow indoors

as it is protected from garden pests which often decimate it outside. Care must be taken not to overuse indoor herbs, otherwise the plant will die from loss of foliage.

Below: Herbs in pots add immediate colour and impact to the garden.

HARVESTING, DRYING & STORING HERBS

In summer when herbs are plentiful, harvest them for using fresh, but also consider picking a supply to preserve for use later in the year. Not all herbs are worth drying though, since some flavours deteriorate with storage.

HARVESTING HERBS

Whatever time of the day you manage to pick herbs for cooking or preserving, their wonderful, aromatic flavour will be sure to enhance the simplest of dishes. Ideally however, herbs are best harvested during the morning, after the dew has evaporated but before the heat of the sun has warmed them. Until then their volatile oils, which provide maximum flavour, are at their most concentrated. As the day progresses the oils start to evaporate into the atmosphere, giving the herb garden such a wonderful fragrance later in the day. Unless you are going to use them immediately, avoid harvesting herbs while it is raining or while they are still wet.

Herb leaves have their most pronounced flavour just before they start to flower, as both the flowers and seeds gradually drain the flavour from the leaves. When picking, try to chop the ends from the straggly stems to keep the plant pruned into a compact, bushy shape. For perennials, particularly young ones or any that have recently been planted, do not pick more than about 10 per cent of the growth so the plants can quickly re-establish themselves.

Below: Twist the leaves of the garlic around string and store in bunches.

Above: Dried bay leaves can be attractively displayed as a wreath.

HARVESTING FLOWERS

Most herb flowers used for cooking or garnishing should be picked when fully opened. Lavender flowers, however, are best picked just as they start to bloom. With all herb flowers, harvest just before they are needed as they tend to wilt quickly, particularly on a warm day and when they are dry.

HARVESTING SEEDS

Seeds from herbs can be harvested for cooking, preserving or replanting. Choose a dry day and snip the entire seed-head into a paper bag. Put in a warm place so that the seeds drop into the bag as they dry. Transfer to a small jar, or, if they are for next season's crop, label the bag and store in a dark, dry place until the spring.

If you have a large herb garden and can afford to gather generous bunches for a constant supply, keep them indoors in a jug (pitcher) or bowl of cold water until you are ready to use them. Replace them as soon as they start to look limp and bedraggled.

DRYING HERBS

Although we tend to consider fresh herbs have a far superior flavour to dried, properly preserved dried herbs

Above: Pick herbs in the morning to help retain the best flavour, tie in bunches and hang up to dry in a warm, dry place out of the sun.

make an excellent substitute for fresh once the plants have died down. Indeed, dried mint is a popular ingredient in some Middle Eastern recipes and dried Greek oregano is often preferred to the fresh for many dishes. Bear in mind when cooking with dried herbs that the flavour is much more concentrated. You will only need about a third of the quantity of dried when substituting for fresh.

Traditionally, herbs for drying were tied in large bunches and left to hang upside-down in the warmth of the kitchen. While this looks attractive and certainly works for short-term use, the herbs will gradually gather dust and moisture from the atmosphere. A very hot kitchen will also destroy the flavour. Better results are achieved by drying herbs on trays or wire racks in a warm place such as an airing cupboard or the oven plate-warming drawer, but definitely not in the sun! Robust herbs

like sage, bay, thyme, oregano, marjoram, mint and rosemary are particularly suited to drying. After a day or two the leaves should be brittle and dry enough to crumble into jars. Cover with lids or cork stoppers and store in a cool, dark place.

FREEZING HERBS

Delicate herbs like basil, parsley, chervil, dill and tarragon are best preserved by freezing. Chop the freshly picked herbs, pack measured quantities in tiny plastic bags and freeze immediately, to preserve maximum flavour. If preferred, basil leaves can be picked from their stems and frozen in a thin layer in a larger bag. You can also make up little bouquet garnis of mixed herbs combining sprigs of bay, parsley and thyme or mixtures of herbs suitable for tomato sauce and pasta dishes. A *fines herbes* blend of parsley, chives, tarragon and chervil is ideal for egg, fish and chicken dishes.

Store all the little bags in a suitable container so that they do not slip to the bottom of the freezer.

SALTED HERBS

Before freezing became popular, herbs were often layered in salt, both to preserve the flavour of the herbs and to flavour the salt. If you would like to do this, use a wide-necked, lidded glass jar and layer the fresh herbs, chopped, or in sprigs, with coarse salt.

COOK'S TIP

Bottles and their lids must be washed and sterilized before using to avoid contaminating the contents. Put dry bottles in the oven set at 150°C/300°F/ Gas 2 for 15 minutes. Sterilize the tops by placing the whole bottle in a pan of water. Bring to the boil and boil for 15 minutes.

HERB DIRECTORY

These herbs appear in the following recipes and many can be grown in a kitchen garden.

ALLIUM CEPA – ONION
Description Single bulbs on each stem.
Cultivation Propagate from sets in early summer or seed sown in spring or autumn. Plant in well-drained soil, rich in nutrients.
Culinary uses Onions are among the most useful herbs. They can be eaten raw, baked, or fried, or cooked in stews, soups, sauces, casseroles or chutneys.

ALLIUM SATIVUM – GARLIC
Description A hardy perennial, often cultivated as an annual. Bulbs are made up of cloves, in a papery, white casing. The clump of flat leaves grows to 60cm/2ft. Flowers are greenish-white, but appear only in warm climates.
Cultivation Plant bulbs in autumn or winter in rich soil and a sunny position. Lift in late summer and dry in the sun before storing. Increase by dividing bulbs and replanting.
Culinary uses Bulbs, separated into cloves are a popular flavouring agent.

ALLIUM SCHOENOPRASUM – CHIVES
Description A hardy perennial with clumps of cylindrical leaves growing from small bulblets to 30cm/12in. Purple flower globes appear in early summer.
Cultivation Need a sunny or semi-shaded position. The leaves do not withstand very cold winters.
Culinary uses A prime culinary herb, it has a milder flavour than its onion cousin. Chop leaves into salads, sauces and soups. Flowers can be used as a garnish.

ANETHUM GRAVEOLENS – DILL
Description An aromatic annual, with a single stem and feathery leaves. It has tiny yellow flowers in midsummer and elliptic fruits. Resembles fennel, but is shorter and has a subtler, less strongly aniseed (anise seed) flavour.
Cultivation Plant dill seeds in well-drained but nutrient-rich soil, in full sun.
Culinary uses Leaves and seeds add a caraway-like flavour to seafood, egg dishes and bland-tasting vegetables. It can be added to curries, rice dishes, soups, pickles and chutneys.

ANTHRISCUS CEREFOLIUM – CHERVIL
Description A hardy annual, with bright-green, finely divided feathery leaves and small, flat, white flowers in early summer.
Cultivation Needs light, moist soil and a sunny situation. Propagate from seed.
Culinary uses The delicate taste of the leaves, which is more distinctive than parsley, complements most dishes. It brings out the flavour of other herbs and is an essential ingredient, along with parsley, tarragon and chives, of the classic French combination, *fines herbes*. It is best used raw.

ARMORACIA RUSTICANA – HORSERADISH
Description A perennial, with large bright-green, oblong leaves, with serrated margins.
Cultivation It flourishes in most soils.
Culinary uses The young, fresh leaves can be added to salads or chopped into smoked-fish pâtés. The fresh root is shredded to make a strong-flavoured, creamy-textured sauce, traditionally served with beef. An excellent accompaniment to cold, smoked meat and fish, hard-boiled (hard-cooked) eggs and stuffed aubergines (eggplant).

ARTEMISIA DRACUNCULUS – FRENCH TARRAGON

Description A perennial with branched stems 1m (1yd) high, and slim leaves.
Cultivation It prefers a fairly moist, but well-drained soil and full sun, and in cold climates needs protection in winter.
Culinary uses It is used in salads, pâté, cooked meat, fish and egg dishes. Well known for its affinity with chicken, it also enhances the flavour of root vegetables. Vinegar flavoured with tarragon is a classic condiment and it is a main ingredient of sauces and stuffings.

BORAGO OFFICINALIS – BORAGE

Description A short-lived hardy annual, with a sprawling habit of growth, hollow, hairy stems, downy leaves and blue (or pink) star-shaped flowers with black centres. It is attractive to bees.
Cultivation Grows in any soil. Prefers a sunny position. Propagate from seed.
Culinary uses The leaves have a faint flavour of cucumbers and are added to soft drinks and wine cups. The flowers make a pretty garnish for salads, and are candied or dried as decorations for sweet dishes and cakes.

BRASSICA NIGRA – MUSTARD

Description An erect annual, with narrow, lobed leaves and bright yellow flowers, followed by pods containing reddish-brown seeds.
Cultivation Requires rich, well-dressed soil and full sun and is propagated by seed sown in spring.
Culinary uses The ground seeds, mixed into a paste, make the familiar "hot-flavoured" condiment. The whole seeds are added to curries, soups, stews, pickles and sauces. Young leaves are eaten with cress, or added to salads.

CAPSICUM ANNUUM var. ANNUUM – BELL OR SWEET PEPPER

Description Annual, which grows into a small bushy plant 60–90cm/2–3ft high, with glossy leaves. Small white flowers are followed by large, sweet, green, ripening to red or yellow, fruits.
Cultivation Frost-tender plant, which must be grown under glass in cool temperate climates. Water freely, feed weekly and mist flowers with water daily to ensure fruit sets.
Culinary uses Fruits are used as vegetables and to flavour savoury dishes.

CAPSICUM FRUTESCENS – CHILLI

Description Most grow into small bushy plants. They have glossy lance-shaped leaves, small white flowers followed by green, ripening to red, fruits.
Cultivation Frost-tender plants, grown under glass in cool temperate climates.
Culinary uses Hot chilli peppers are added to pickles and chutneys; dried to make cayenne pepper, chilli powder or paprika.

CARUM CARVI – CARAWAY

Description A biennial 45–60cm/ 18–24in tall, with feathery leaves. In its second year, umbels of white flowers are followed by ridged fruits, which are popularly known as seeds.
Cultivation Prefers well-drained soil and a sunny position. Propagated from seed sown in spring, preferably in situ.
Culinary uses Seeds are used to flavour cakes, breads, cheese, baked apples, cabbage and meat dishes. Also used as a pickling spice.

CINNAMOMUM ZEYLANICUM – CINNAMON

Description A medium-sized evergreen tree growing to about 9m/30ft, with brown, papery bark. The inner bark of young stems is wrapped round thin rods to form quills.
Cultivation Grows in sandy soils, and needs plenty of rain, sun and a minimum temperature of 15°C/59°F.
Culinary uses A popular spice for savoury and sweet dishes, it is also a traditional ingredient for Christmas puddings, mince pies and spiced drinks.

CITRUS LIMON – LEMON

Description A small evergreen tree, with light-green, oval leaves and thorny stems. Clusters of white flowers are followed by bitter-tasting yellow fruits.
Cultivation Requires well-drained, not too acid compost – 6–6.5pH – and protection from frost.
Culinary uses The juice and rind of the fruit are widely used as a flavouring in cooking, and in soft drinks, sauces, pickles, preserves and marinades. The zest of lemon, containing its oil, gives the strongest flavour.

CORIANDRUM SATIVUM – CORIANDER (CILANTRO)

Description An annual with pungent leaves. Small white flowers are followed by pale-brown fruits (seeds).
Cultivation Propagated from seed.
Culinary uses The leaves have a stronger, spicier taste than the seeds. Both are used in curries, pickles and chutneys, also in Middle Eastern, Indian, South-east Asian and South American cuisines. Leaves are added to salads, seeds are used in sweet dishes, breads and cakes, and to flavour liqueurs.

CROCUS SATIVUS – SAFFRON

Description A perennial with linear leaves growing from a rounded corm. Fragrant lilac flowers appear in autumn, the red anthers of which produce the saffron threads.
Cultivation Needs well-drained soil, sun and warm summers to flower.
Culinary uses Saffron is widely used as a flavouring and colourant in Middle Eastern and northern Indian cookery, in rice dishes and fish soups. It is sometimes used in sweets and cakes.

CURCUMA LONGA – TURMERIC

Description A perennial with shiny, lanceolate leaves and spikes of pale-yellow flowers.
Cultivation A tender, tropical plant, it requires well-drained but moist soil, a humid atmosphere and minimum temperatures of 15–18°C/59–64°F.
Culinary uses The rhizomes are boiled, skinned, dried and ground into powder. This is used in Worcestershire sauce and curry powder, and adds colour and a musky flavour to savoury dishes.

CYMBOPOGON CITRATUS – LEMON GRASS

Description A tall, clump-forming perennial, it has linear, grass-like leaves, strongly scented with lemon.
Cultivation In cool, temperate climates it must be grown as a conservatory (porch) or warm greenhouse plant, and moved outside in the summer.
Culinary uses The young white stem and leaf base are chopped and used in stir-fry dishes, also in Thai, Malaysian and South-east Asian cuisine. Leaves may also be infused (steeped) to make tea.

ELETTARIA CARDAMOMUM – CARDAMOM
Description A large perennial, with a clump of leaves growing from a fleshy rhizome. Flowers are followed by pale green capsules, which contain many small pungent black seeds.
Cultivation Needs a minimum temperature of 18°C/64°F, well-drained, rich soil, partial shade, plenty of rain and high humidity.
Culinary uses A major curry spice, the seeds are also used to flavour hot wine punches, sweet, milky rice puddings and egg custard.

ERUCA VESICARIA subsp SATIVA – ROCKET (ARUGULA)
Description A frost-hardy annual, with dentate, deeply divided leaves. Small, four-petalled, white flowers, streaked at the centre of each petal with violet, appear in late winter to early summer.
Cultivation Propagate from seed, from late winter to early summer. Grow on poor, dry soil, with plenty of sun, for a more pungent taste.
Culinary uses The pungent leaves lend interest to lettuce, and other bland-tasting leaves, as a salad ingredient.

FICUS CARICA – FIG
Description A deciduous tree. The flowers are completely concealed within fleshy receptacles and are followed by small, pear-shaped fruits.
Cultivation Warm, sunny summers are necessary to produce fruit. Grow in well-drained, rich soil.
Culinary uses The fruits are delicious raw, or as a cooked ingredient of sweet pies, pastries, desserts and conserves. Dried figs can be stewed, or eaten as they are. They are also used in cakes.

FOENICULUM – FENNEL
Description An aromatic perennial, with erect, hollow stems and mid-green, feathery foliage. Umbels of yellow flowers are borne in summer, followed by ovoid, ridged, yellow-green seeds. The plant is scented with aniseed.
Cultivation Propagation is from seed sown in spring.
Culinary uses Leaves and seeds go well with fish, especially oily fish. Seeds add flavour to stir-fry and rice dishes. The bulbous stems of fennel are eaten raw in salads or cooked as a vegetable.

FRAGARIA VESCA – WILD STRAWBERRY
Description A low-growing perennial. It has shiny, trifoliate leaves, and small white, yellow-centred flowers, followed by red ovoid fruits with tiny yellow seeds embedded in the surface.
Cultivation Grow in fertile, well-drained soil (alkaline), in sun or partial shade.
Culinary uses Rich in vitamin C, fruits are eaten fresh or made into desserts, conserves and juices. Dried leaves are included in blended herbal teas to improve taste and aroma.

HELIANTHUS – SUNFLOWER
Description A tall annual, up to 3m/10ft in height, with erect stems and oval, hairy leaves. The daisy-shaped flower heads, and brown disc florets at the centre, are followed by the striped black-and-white seeds, about 1,000 per head.
Cultivation Propagate by seed in spring.
Culinary uses Seeds are eaten fresh or roasted in salads and breads. Oil, made from the seeds, is used for cooking and in salad dressings. It is also a constituent of margarine.

JUGLANS REGIA – WALNUT
Description A deciduous tree bearing catkins, which are followed by dark green fruits, each containing a wrinkled brown walnut.
Cultivation Requires deep, rich soil and a sunny position.
Culinary uses Walnuts are included in many dishes, sweet and savoury, for their distinctive flavour.

LAURUS NOBILIS – BAY
Description An evergreen shrub, or small tree, it has aromatic dark-green, glossy ovate leaves.
Cultivation Grow in fertile, reasonably moist but well-drained soil in a sheltered, sunny position.
Culinary uses A first-rate culinary herb, a bay leaf is always included in a bouquet garni, and adds flavour to marinades, casseroles, stews, soups and dishes requiring a long cooking time. Also used to flavour sweet sauces and as a garnish for citrus sorbets.

LAVANDULA ANGUSTIFOLIA – LAVENDER
Description An evergreen shrub with slender leaves from silvery white to green in colour and mauve to purple flower clusters held on long stems.
Cultivation Requires a well-drained soil and plenty of sun.
Culinary uses Flowers are used to flavour sugar for making cakes, biscuits, meringues, ice creams and desserts. They can be added to vinegar, marmalade or jam, or cooked (tied in a muslin bag) with blackcurrants or fruit mixtures.

LEVISTICUM OFFICINALE – LOVAGE
Description A hardy herbaceous perennial, growing on deep fleshy roots, it has glossy leaves with a spicy, celery-like scent, and umbels of dull-yellow flowers in summer, followed by seeds.
Cultivation A vigorous, spreading plant.
Culinary uses Leaves are used to flavour soups, stews, meat, fish or vegetable dishes; young shoots and stems are eaten as a vegetable (like braised celery) and may be candied; seeds are added to biscuits and bread.

MELISSA OFFICINALIS – LEMON BALM
Description A vigorous, bushy perennial, it has strongly lemon-scented, rough-textured, leaves. Clusters of pale-yellow flowers appear in late summer.
Cultivation Grows in any soil in sun or partial shade.
Culinary uses Leaves are best used fresh, as scent and therapeutic properties are lost when dried and stored. They add a lemon flavour to desserts, cordials, liqueurs and wine cups, salads, soups, sauces, stuffings, poultry, game and fish.

MYRISTICA FRAGRANS – NUTMEG
Description Evergreen tree bearing yellow globular fruits, which contain the nutmeg.
Cultivation These tropical trees require sandy, humus-rich soil and shade or partial shade. May be grown in a conservatory (greenhouse) with a minimum temperature of 18°C/64°F and humid atmosphere.
Culinary uses Ground or grated (shredded) nutmeg is used in a wide range of sweet and savoury dishes, including soups, sauces, milk and cheese dishes, fruit cakes, puddings and drinks.

MYRRHIS ODORATA – SWEET CICELY

Description A vigorous, hardy, herbaceous perennial, with a strong taproot, with hollow stems and soft, downy, fern-like leaves. Compound umbels of white flowers appear in late spring, followed by large, distinctively beaked and ridged brown fruit. The whole plant is pleasantly scented.

Cultivation Sew seeds in autumn.

Culinary uses Traditionally used as a sweetening agent and flavouring for stewed soft fruits and rhubarb. Leaves also make a pretty garnish for sweet and savoury dishes.

OCIMUM BASILICUM – BASIL

Description Basil is a half-hardy annual with oval, pale-green leaves. A purple-leaved variety is also available.

Cultivation It requires well-drained, moist, medium-rich soil and full sun. Basil is propagated from seed, and flourishes as a container plant.

Culinary uses Fresh leaves should be added towards the end of the cooking process so that its fragrance is not lost. They have an affinity with tomatoes and aubergines (eggplant), and add fragrance to ratatouille, pasta sauces, pesto sauce and pizza toppings.

OLEA EUROPAEA – OLIVE

Description An evergreen tree, with smooth, leathery, grey-green leaves. Creamy-white flowers are borne in summer, followed by fruits.

Cultivation Requires dry soil and full sun.

Culinary uses The fruits are eaten as appetizers, added to salads, sauces, bread, pizzas and pasta. The oil, pressed from the fruit, is used in salad dressings, sauces, mayonnaise and as a cooking oil. Extra-virgin, cold-pressed oil, has the best flavour and properties.

ORIGANUM MAJORANA – SWEET MARJORAM

Description Half-hardy perennial. Has greyish-green leaves and small, white, sometimes pinkish flowers in knot-like clusters surrounding the stem.

Cultivation Requires well-drained, fertile soil and full sun. Sow seed in spring, after danger of frost has passed.

Culinary uses Leaves and flowering stems are used to flavour savoury dishes, especially pasta sauces, pizza toppings, bread, oil and vinegar.

ORIGANUM VULGARE – OREGANO

Description A bushy, hardy perennial, with aromatic, ovate, dark-green leaves and panicles of pink to purple tubular flowers in summer.

Cultivation Requires well-drained soil and a sunny position.

Culinary uses Leaves are widely used in Italian, Greek and Mediterranean cuisine, especially in pasta sauces, pizza toppings, tomato sauces, vegetable dishes and to flavour bread, oil and vinegars.

PAPAVER SOMNIFERUM – OPIUM POPPY

Description A hardy annual, it has oblong, deeply lobed, blue-green leaves. Large, lilac, pink or white flowers, with papery petals, in early summer, followed by blue-green seed pods.

Cultivation Propagated by seed sown in spring, often self-seeds.

Culinary uses The seeds are dried for use whole or ground in breads, biscuits, bakery products and as a garnish. Commercially produced seed is from a subspecies of *Papaver somniferum*.

PETROSELINUM – PARSLEY

Description A frost-hardy biennial, growing to 30–60cm/1–2ft.

Cultivation Parsley requires rich, moist but well-drained soil and a sunny position, or partial shade.

Culinary uses The leaves are added to salads, sauces, salad dressings, savoury butter, stuffings, chopped into meat, fish and vegetable dishes and used as a garnish. The stalks are essential to a bouquet garni for flavouring casseroles.

PIPER NIGRUM – BLACK PEPPER

Description A perennial climber, with ovate, prominently-veined, dark-green leaves. Black pepper is produced from whole fruits, picked and dried just as they start to go red; white pepper is from ripe fruits, and green pepper is from unripe pickled fruits.

Cultivation Pepper requires deep, rich, manured soil, plenty of water, a humid atmosphere and a shady position.

Culinary uses The fruits are chiefly used as a condiment and flavouring in a wide range of dishes.

ROSA – ROSE

Description Flowering shrub.

Cultivation Fertile, moist soil and a sunny position are best for producing thriving rose plants with large flowers.

Culinary uses Hips, from R. *canina*, are used for making vinegar, syrups, preserves and wines. Flower petals, from R. *gallica*, are added to salads and desserts, crystallized, made into jellies, jams and conserves. Distilled rose water is used to flavour confectionery and desserts, especially in Middle Eastern dishes.

ROSMARINUS OFFICINALIS – ROSEMARY

Description An evergreen shrub, it has woody branches and strongly aromatic, needle-like foliage. A dense covering of small, tubular, flowers, appear in spring.

Cultivation Needs well-drained soil and a sunny position.

Culinary uses The leaves are a classic flavouring for roasted lamb, stews and casseroles, and added to marinades, vinegar, oil and dressings. Used sparingly, the leaves and flowers add spice and interest to cakes, biscuits, sorbets and stewed apples.

RUMEX ACETOSA – SORREL

Description A hardy perennial with large, pale-green, oblong to lanceolate leaves, and large terminal spikes of small, disc-shaped, reddish-brown flowers on long stalks.

Cultivation Grows best and runs to seed less quickly in rich, moist soil, in a sunny or partially shady position.

Culinary uses Young sorrel leaves add a pleasant, lemony flavour to soups, sauces, salads, egg and cheese dishes. They have the best flavour and texture in spring.

SALVIA OFFICINALIS – SAGE

Description An evergreen, highly aromatic, shrubby perennial.

Cultivation Grow in light, well-drained soil in full sun.

Culinary uses Leaves, fresh or dried, are used to give flavour to Mediterranean dishes, cheese, sausages, goose, pork and other fatty meat. In Italy sage is added to liver dishes. It is also made into stuffings – a classic combination is sage and onion. Leaves of pineapple sage may be floated in drinks.

SAMBUCUS NIGRA – ELDERFLOWER

Description Small deciduous tree, which bears flat umbels of creamy, musk-scented flowers in early summer followed by clusters of black fruit in early autumn.

Cultivation Prefers moist but well-drained, humus-rich soil in sun or partial shade.

Culinary uses Fresh or dried flowers give a muscatel flavour to gooseberries and stewed fruits and are added to desserts and sorbets. Flowers and berries are used in vinegars, cordials and wines.

SANGUISORBA MINOR – SALAD BURNET

Description A clump-forming perennial, it has pinnate leaves with numerous pairs of oval, serrated-edged leaflets and long stalks topped by rounded crimson flower-heads.

Cultivation Thrives on chalk (alkaline). Propagated by seed sown in spring.

Culinary uses The leaves have a mild, cucumber flavour, make a pleasant addition to salads and can be floated in drinks or wine punch.

SATUREJA HORTENSIS – SUMMER SAVORY

Description A small, bushy, hardy annual, it has woody stems and small, leathery, dark-green leaves. Tiny white or pale-lilac flowers appear in summer.

Cultivation Grow in well-drained soil in full sun. Propagated from seed sown in early spring.

Culinary uses Summer savory has an affinity with beans. The leaves add a spicy flavour to dried herb mixtures, stuffings, pulses, pâtés and meat dishes.

THYMUS VULGARIS – THYME

Description Common thyme is a fine-stemmed, low-growing sub-shrub with tiny leaves. Pale mauve flowers are borne in summer. There are many other species of thyme with differing flavours.

Cultivation All thymes require free-draining, gritty soil and a sunny position.

Culinary uses The leaves, fresh or dried, are widely used as a culinary flavouring in marinades, meat dishes, soups, stews and casseroles.

TROPAEOLUM MAJUS – NASTURTIUM

Description In cool temperate regions it is a half-hardy annual. Yellow or orange flowers grow on stalks.

Cultivation Grow in relatively poor soil for the best production of flowers. Easily propagated from seed sown in containers, or in situ, in spring.

Culinary uses The leaves are added to salads for their peppery taste. Flowers are also used as a flavouring for vinegar. Seeds, when still green, are pickled as a substitute for capers.

ZINGIBER OFFICINALE – GINGER

Description A perennial reed-like plant with branching rhizomes, growing to 1–1.2m/3–4ft high.

Cultivation Tender, tropical plant requiring fertile, humus-rich, well-drained soil with plenty of moisture and humidity.

Culinary uses Fresh ginger is grated (shredded) and added to stir-fry dishes, and widely used, fresh or dried, in Chinese and Thai cooking. Dried ground ginger is an ingredient of curry powder, pickles and chutneys. It is also used in biscuits, cakes and desserts.

soups, salads & appetizers

Aromatic herbs like dill, basil, saffron and fennel can be stirred into lightly

cooked summer soups or more robust wintry ones to create a fabulous

blend of colour and flavour. Stunning salads, from cooling leafy ones to

those based on bulgur wheat or potatoes, come to life with an intensely

flavoured herb dressing. Just as easy is a roasted garlic pâté, mashed

with rosemary, thyme and goat's cheese for a memorable appetizer. This

chapter has ideas you'll come back to time

and time again.

SORREL, SPINACH AND DILL SOUP

THE WARM FLAVOUR OF HORSERADISH AND THE ANISEED FLAVOUR OF DILL MELD WITH SORREL AND SPINACH TO MAKE THIS UNUSUAL RUSSIAN SOUP. AN EXCELLENT SUMMER SOUP, SERVED CHILLED.

SERVES SIX

INGREDIENTS

25g/1oz/2 tbsp butter
225g/8oz sorrel, stalks removed
225g/8oz young spinach,
  stalks removed
25g/1oz fresh horseradish, grated
  (shredded)
750ml/1¼ pints/3 cups cider
1 pickled cucumber, finely chopped
30ml/2 tbsp chopped fresh dill
225g/8oz cooked fish, such as pike,
  perch or salmon, skinned and boned
salt and ground black pepper
sprig of dill, to garnish

1 Melt the butter in a large pan. Add the prepared sorrel and spinach leaves together with the grated fresh horseradish. Cover the pan and allow to cook gently for 3–4 minutes, or until the sorrel and spinach leaves have wilted.

2 Tip into a food processor or blender and process to a fine purée (paste). Ladle into a tureen or bowl and stir in the cider, cucumber and dill.

3 Chop the fish into bitesize pieces. Add to the soup, then season well. Chill for at least 3 hours before serving, garnished with a sprig of dill.

MELON AND BASIL SOUP

BASIL AND LIME GIVE ZEST TO SWEET MELON IN THIS CHILLED SUMMER SOUP. SIMPLE TO PREPARE, BUT STRIKINGLY UNUSUAL, IT MAKES A PERFECT START TO A SUMMER MEAL.

3 Place the sugar, water and lime rind in a small pan over a low heat. Stir until dissolved, then bring to the boil and simmer for 2–3 minutes.

4 Remove the pan from the heat and leave to cool slightly. Pour half the mixture into the food processor or blender with the melon flesh. Blend until smooth, adding the remaining syrup and lime juice to taste.

5 Pour the mixture into a bowl, then stir in the basil.

6 Cover the bowl with clear film and transfer to the refrigerator to chill for 2–3 hours. When ready to serve, pour into individual bowls and serve garnished with basil leaves and melon balls.

SERVES FOUR TO SIX

INGREDIENTS
2 Charentais or cantaloupe melons
75g/3oz/6 tbsp caster
  (superfine) sugar
175ml/6fl oz/¾ cup water
finely grated (shredded) rind and
  juice of 1 lime
45ml/3 tbsp finely chopped
  fresh basil
fresh basil leaves, to garnish

1 Cut the melons in half across the middle. Scrape out the seeds with a spoon and discard.

2 Using a melon baller, scoop out 20–24 balls and set aside for the garnish. Scoop out the remaining flesh and place in the bowl of a food processor or blender.

COOK'S TIP
Add the syrup in two stages, as the amount of sugar needed will depend on the sweetness of the melon.

CUCUMBER AND GARLIC SOUP WITH WALNUTS

YOGURT AND CUCUMBER MAKE REFRESHING PARTNERS FOR CHILLED SOUP. HERE, THE FAMILIAR COMBINATION IS GIVEN A RICHER DIMENSION USING PUNGENT GARLIC AND DILL.

SERVES FIVE TO SIX

INGREDIENTS
½ cucumber
4 garlic cloves, peeled but left whole
2.5ml/½ tsp salt
75g/3oz/¾ cup walnut pieces
40g/1½oz day-old bread, torn
   into pieces
30ml/2 tbsp walnut or sunflower oil
400ml/14fl oz/1⅔ cups natural
   (plain) yogurt
120ml/4fl oz/½ cup cold water or
   chilled still mineral water
5–10ml/1–2 tsp lemon juice
For the garnish
40g/1½oz/scant ⅓ cup coarsely
   chopped walnuts
25ml/1½ tbsp olive oil
sprigs of fresh dill

1 Dice the cucumber flesh and set aside.

2 Using a large mortar and pestle, crush the garlic cloves and salt together well. Add the walnut and bread pieces and crush everything together until the consistency is smooth.

3 Add the walnut or sunflower oil slowly, and use the pestle to combine the mixture well.

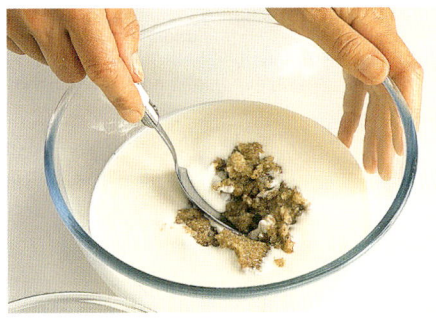

4 Transfer the mixture into a large bowl and beat in the yogurt and the diced cucumber flesh.

5 Add the cold water or mineral water and lemon juice to taste, then pour the soup into chilled bowls to serve. Garnish with the coarsely chopped walnuts, a little olive oil drizzled over the nuts and sprigs of fresh dill.

COOK'S TIP
If you prefer your soup to be smooth, purée it in a food processor or blender before serving.

SHERRIED ONION AND SAFFRON SOUP WITH ALMONDS

THE SPANISH COMBINATION OF ONIONS, GARLIC, SAFFRON AND SHERRY GIVES THIS PALE YELLOW SOUP A BEGUILING FLAVOUR THAT MAKES IT THE PERFECT OPENING COURSE FOR A SPECIAL MEAL.

SERVES FOUR

INGREDIENTS

40g/1½oz/3 tbsp butter
2 large yellow onions, thinly sliced
1 small garlic clove, finely chopped
good pinch of saffron threads
50g/2oz/⅓ cup blanched almonds,
    toasted and finely ground
750ml/1¼ pints/3 cups good chicken
    or vegetable stock
45ml/3 tbsp dry sherry
salt and ground black pepper
30ml/2 tbsp toasted flaked (sliced)
    almonds and chopped fresh parsley,
    to garnish

1 Melt the butter in a heavy pan over a low heat. Add the onions and garlic, stirring to coat them thoroughly in the butter. Cover the pan and cook very gently, stirring frequently, for 15–20 minutes, or until the onions are soft and golden yellow.

COOK'S TIP

This soup is also delicious served chilled. Add a little more chicken or vegetable stock to make a slightly thinner soup, then leave to cool and chill for at least 4 hours (or overnight). Just before serving, taste for seasoning. Float one or two ice cubes in each bowl.

2 Add the saffron threads and cook, uncovered, for 3–4 minutes, then add the ground almonds and continue to cook, stirring constantly, for another 2–3 minutes.

3 Pour in the chicken or vegetable stock and sherry and stir in 5ml/1 tsp salt. Season with plenty of black pepper. Bring the mixture to the boil, then lower the heat and simmer gently for about 10 minutes.

4 Process the soup in a food processor or blender until smooth, then return it to the rinsed pan. Reheat slowly, without allowing the soup to boil, stirring occasionally. Taste for seasoning, adding more salt and ground black pepper if required.

5 Ladle the soup into four heated bowls, garnish with the toasted flaked almonds and chopped fresh parsley, and serve immediately.

CAULIFLOWER AND BEAN SOUP WITH FENNEL SEED AND PARSLEY

FENNEL SEEDS SAUTÉED WITH GARLIC AND ONION GIVE A DELICIOUS EDGE TO THE MILD FLAVOURS OF CAULIFLOWER AND FLAGEOLET BEANS IN THIS SUBSTANTIAL AND WARMING SOUP.

SERVES FOUR TO SIX

INGREDIENTS
    15ml/1 tbsp olive oil
    1 garlic clove, crushed
    1 onion, chopped
    10ml/2 tsp fennel seeds
    1 cauliflower, cut into small florets
    2 × 400g/14oz cans flageolet or
      cannellini beans, drained and rinsed
    1.2 litres/2 pints/5 cups vegetable
      stock or water
    60–90ml/4–6 tbsp chopped fresh
      parsley
    salt and ground black pepper
    toasted slices of French bread,
      to serve

1 Heat the olive oil in a large, flameproof casserole or heavy pan. Add the garlic, onion and fennel seeds and cook them gently for 5 minutes, or until they are softened.

2 Add the cauliflower florets and half of the flageolet beans and pour in the stock or water.

3 Bring to the boil. Reduce the heat and simmer for 10 minutes, or until the cauliflower is tender.

4 Pour the soup into a food processor or blender and blend until smooth. Return to the pan, and stir in the remaining flageolet beans. Season to taste.

5 Reheat the soup and pour into bowls. Sprinkle with chopped parsley and serve with toasted slices of French bread.

ROASTED PEPPER AND ONION SOUP

GRILLING INTENSIFIES THE FLAVOUR OF SWEET RED AND YELLOW BELL PEPPERS AND HELPS THIS SOUP KEEP ITS STUNNING COLOUR. THE GARLIC AND ONION ADD CHARACTER. PEPPERS ARE NOW AVAILABLE ALL YEAR ROUND AND MAKE A BRIGHT AND WELCOME SOUP WHATEVER THE TIME OF YEAR.

SERVES FOUR

INGREDIENTS
    3 red (bell) peppers
    1 yellow (bell) pepper
    1 onion, chopped
    1 garlic clove, crushed
    750ml/1¼ pints/3 cups good
        vegetable stock
    15ml/1 tbsp plain (all-purpose) flour
    salt and ground black pepper
    red and yellow (bell) peppers diced,
        to garnish

1 Preheat the grill (broiler). Halve the peppers and cut out their stalks and white pith. Scrape out the seeds.

2 Line a grill (broiling) pan with foil and arrange the halved peppers, skin-side up, in a single layer. Grill (broil) until the skins have blackened and blistered.

VARIATION
If preferred, garnish the soup with a swirl of natural (plain) yogurt instead of sprinkling it with the diced bell peppers.

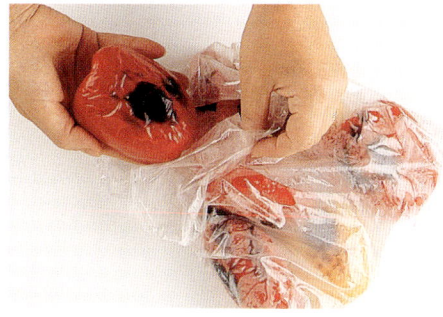

3 Transfer the peppers to a plastic bag. Seal and leave until cool, then peel away their skins and discard. Roughly chop the pepper flesh.

4 Put the onion and garlic clove into a large pan with 150ml/¼ pint/⅔ cup stock. Boil for about 5 minutes, or until most of the stock has reduced. Lower the heat and stir until softened and just beginning to colour.

5 Sprinkle the flour over the onions, then gradually stir in the remaining stock. Add the chopped, roasted peppers and bring to the boil. Cover and simmer for a further 5 minutes.

6 Leave to cool slightly, then purée in a food processor or blender. Season to taste. Return to the pan and reheat until piping hot. Ladle into four soup bowls and garnish with diced peppers.

ROASTED TOMATO AND MOZZARELLA SALAD WITH BASIL DRESSING

FRESH BASIL MAKES AN APPETIZING AND VIVIDLY COLOURED OIL FOR SERVING WITH MOZZARELLA AND TOMATOES. ROASTING THE TOMATOES BRINGS OUT THEIR FLAVOUR AND ADDS A NEW DIMENSION TO THIS SALAD.

SERVES FOUR

INGREDIENTS
    olive oil, for brushing
    6 large plum tomatoes
    2 balls fresh mozzarella cheese,
      cut into 8–12 slices
    salt and ground black pepper
    basil leaves, to garnish
For the basil oil
    25 basil leaves
    60ml/4 tbsp extra virgin olive oil
    1 garlic clove, crushed

COOK'S TIP
Make the basil oil just before serving to retain its fresh flavour and bright colour.

1 Preheat the oven to 200°C/400°F/ Gas 6 and oil a baking tray. Cut the tomatoes in half lengthways and remove the seeds. Place skin-side down on the baking tray and roast for 20 minutes, or until the tomatoes are tender but still retain their shape.

2 Meanwhile, make the basil oil. Place the basil leaves, olive oil and garlic in a food processor or blender and process until smooth. Transfer to a bowl and chill until required.

3 For each serving, place the tomato halves on top of two or three slices of mozzarella and drizzle over the oil. Season well. Garnish with basil leaves and serve at once.

COOK'S TIP
The best mozzarella to use for this salad is the traditional kind made from buffalo's milk, which has the best flavour.

MIXED HERB SALAD WITH TOASTED SUNFLOWER AND PUMPKIN SEEDS

THE FUSION OF CORIANDER, PARSLEY, BASIL AND ROCKET WITH SUNFLOWER AND PUMPKIN SEEDS GIVES THIS SALAD ITS CRUNCHY AND CRISPY TEXTURES.

SERVES FOUR

INGREDIENTS
    25g/1oz/3 tbsp pumpkin seeds
    25g/1oz/3 tbsp sunflower seeds
    90g/3½oz mixed salad leaves
    50g/2oz/2 cups mixed salad herbs,
      such as coriander (cilantro), parsley,
      basil and rocket (arugula)
For the dressing
    60ml/4 tbsp extra virgin olive oil
    15ml/1 tbsp balsamic vinegar
    2.5ml/½ tsp Dijon mustard
    salt and ground black pepper

COOK'S TIP
Use your hands to toss the salad to avoid bruising the leaves.

1 To make the dressing, combine the ingredients in a bowl or screw-top jar, and shake or mix with a small whisk or fork until combined.

2 Toast the pumpkin and sunflower seeds in a dry frying pan over a medium heat for 2 minutes, or until golden, tossing frequently to prevent them burning. Allow to cool slightly.

3 Put the salad and herb leaves in a large bowl and then sprinkle with the cooled seeds.

4 Pour the dressing over the salad and toss carefully until the leaves are well coated, then serve.

CUCUMBER AND DILL SALAD

AROMATIC DILL IS A PARTICULARLY USEFUL HERB TO USE WITH SALADS. HERE, ITS ANISEED FLAVOUR IS PARTNERED WITH FRESH-TASTING CUCUMBER IN A SOUR CREAM DRESSING.

3 Rinse well under cold running water, then pat dry with kitchen paper.

4 Finely chop about 45ml/3 tbsp fresh dill, setting aside one sprig for the garnish. Put the slices of cucumber in a bowl, add the chopped dill and combine the ingredients together, either mixing with your hands or with a fork.

5 In another bowl, stir the vinegar into the sour cream and season the mixture with pepper.

SERVES FOUR

INGREDIENTS
2 cucumbers
5ml/1 tsp salt
5 sprigs fresh dill
15ml/1 tbsp white wine vinegar
150ml/¼ pint/⅔ cup sour cream
ground black pepper

1 Use a cannelle knife (zester) to peel away strips of rind from along the length of the cucumbers, creating a striped effect. Slice thinly.

2 Put the slices in a sieve or colander set over a bowl and sprinkle with the salt. Leave for 1 hour to drain.

6 Pour the sour cream over the cucumber and chill for 1 hour before turning into a serving dish. Garnish with the sprig of dill, and serve.

COOK'S TIP
Salting the cucumber draws out some of the moisture, thereby making it firmer. Make sure you rinse it thoroughly before using or the salad will be too salty.

FENNEL, ORANGE AND ROCKET SALAD

AN UNUSUAL COMBINATION OF FENNEL, ROCKET, ORANGE AND OLIVES IS BROUGHT TOGETHER IN THIS REFRESHING SALAD THAT IS IDEAL SERVED WITH SPICY OR RICH FOOD.

SERVES FOUR

INGREDIENTS
    2 oranges
    1 fennel bulb
    115g/4oz rocket (arugula) leaves
    50g/2oz/⅓ cup black olives
For the dressing
    30ml/2 tbsp extra virgin olive oil
    15ml/1 tbsp balsamic vinegar
    1 small garlic clove, crushed
    salt and ground black pepper

1 With a vegetable peeler, cut strips of rind from the oranges, leaving the pith behind, and cut into thin julienne strips. Cook in boiling water for a few minutes. Drain. Peel the oranges, removing all the white pith. Slice them into thin rounds and discard any seeds.

2 Cut the fennel bulb in half lengthways with a sharp knife and slice across the bulb as thinly as possible, preferably in a food processor fitted with a slicing disc or using a mandolin.

3 Combine the oranges and fennel slices in a serving bowl and toss with the rocket leaves.

4 To make the dressing, mix together the olive oil, balsamic vinegar, crushed garlic and seasoning and pour over the salad in the bowl.

5 Toss the salad ingredients together well and leave to stand for a few minutes. Sprinkle with the black olives and julienne strips of orange rind.

Fennel and Egg Tabbouleh with Herbs

Tabbouleh is a Middle Eastern salad of steamed bulgur wheat, flavoured with lots of parsley, mint, lemon juice and garlic. Here, the salad also includes the sweet, aniseed flavour of fennel and the tang of black olives.

SERVES FOUR

INGREDIENTS

250g/9oz/1⅓ cups bulgur wheat
4 small eggs
1 fennel bulb
1 bunch of spring onions (scallions), chopped
25g/1oz/½ cup drained sun-dried tomatoes in oil, sliced
45ml/3 tbsp chopped fresh parsley
30ml/2 tbsp chopped fresh mint
75g/3oz/½ cup black olives
60ml/4 tbsp olive oil
30ml/2 tbsp garlic oil
30ml/2 tbsp lemon juice
50g/2oz/½ cup chopped hazelnuts, toasted
1 open-textured loaf or 4 pitta breads, warmed
salt and ground black pepper

1 In a bowl, pour boiling water over the bulgur wheat, and leave to soak for about 15 minutes.

2 Drain the bulgur wheat in a metal sieve, and place the sieve over a pan of boiling water. Cover and steam for about 10 minutes. Fluff up the grains with a fork and spread out on a metal tray. Set aside to cool.

3 Hard-boil (hard-cook) the eggs for 8 minutes. Cool under running water, peel and quarter.

4 Halve and finely slice the fennel. Boil in salted water for 6 minutes, then drain and cool under running water.

5 Combine the eggs, fennel, spring onions, sun-dried tomatoes, parsley, mint and olives with the bulgur wheat. Dress with olive oil, garlic oil and lemon juice, then add the nuts. Season well, then tear the bread into pieces and add to the salad. Serve immediately.

COOK'S TIP

If you are short of time, simply soak the bulgur wheat in boiling water for about 20 minutes. Drain and rinse under cold water to cool, then drain thoroughly.

POTATO AND MUSSEL SALAD WITH SHALLOT AND CHIVE DRESSING

SHALLOT AND CHIVES IN A CREAMY DRESSING ADD BITE TO THIS SALAD OF POTATO AND SWEET MUSSELS AND PARSLEY. SERVE WITH FULL-FLAVOURED WATERCRESS AND PLENTY OF WHOLEMEAL BREAD.

SERVES FOUR

INGREDIENTS
  675g/1½lb salad potatoes
  1kg/2¼lb mussels, scrubbed and
    beards removed
  200ml/7fl oz/scant 1 cup dry
    white wine
  15g/½oz/¼ cup chopped flat
    leaf parsley
  salt and ground black pepper
  chopped fresh chives or chive
    flowers, to garnish
For the dressing
  105ml/7 tbsp mild olive oil
  15–30ml/1–2 tbsp white
    wine vinegar
  5ml/1 tsp Dijon mustard
  1 large shallot, very finely chopped
  15ml/1 tbsp chopped fresh chives
  45ml/3 tbsp double (heavy) cream
  pinch of caster (superfine) sugar

1 Cook the potatoes in boiling, salted water for 15–20 minutes, or until tender. Drain, cool, then peel. Slice the potatoes into a bowl and toss with 30ml/2 tbsp of the oil for the dressing.

2 Discard any open mussels that do not close when sharply tapped. Bring the white wine to the boil in a large, heavy pan. Add the mussels, cover and boil vigorously, shaking the pan occasionally, for 3–4 minutes, or until the mussels have opened. Discard any mussels which have not opened after 5 minutes' cooking. Drain and shell the mussels, reserving the cooking liquid.

3 Boil the reserved cooking liquid until reduced to about 45ml/3 tbsp. Strain this through a fine sieve over the potatoes and toss to mix.

4 For the dressing, whisk together the remaining oil, 15ml/1 tbsp vinegar, the mustard, shallot and chives.

5 Add the cream and whisk again to form a thick dressing. Adjust the seasoning, adding more vinegar and a pinch of sugar to taste.

6 Toss the mussels with the potatoes, then mix in the dressing and chopped parsley. Serve sprinkled with chopped chives or chive flowers separated into florets.

COOK'S TIP
Potato salads, such as this one, should not be chilled if at all possible as the cold alters the texture of the potatoes and of the creamy dressing. For the best flavour and texture, serve this salad just cool or at room temperature.

SALAD OF FRESH CEPS WITH PARSLEY AND WALNUT DRESSING

THE DISTINCTIVE FLAVOUR OF WALNUTS IS A NATURAL PARTNER TO MUSHROOMS. HERE, WILD MUSHROOMS AND WALNUTS MELD WITH FRENCH MUSTARD, LEMON, PARSLEY AND NUT OILS IN A RICHLY FLAVOURED SALAD.

SERVES FOUR

INGREDIENTS
   350g/12oz/4¾ cups fresh small
      cep mushrooms
   50g/2oz/½ cup broken walnut pieces
   175g/6oz mixed salad leaves, to
      include Batavia, young spinach
      and frisée
   50g/2oz/⅔ cup freshly shaved
      Parmesan cheese
   salt and ground black pepper
For the dressing
   2 egg yolks
   2.5ml/½ tsp French mustard
   75ml/5 tbsp groundnut (peanut) oil
   45ml/3 tbsp walnut oil
   30ml/2 tbsp lemon juice
   30ml/2 tbsp chopped fresh parsley
   1 pinch caster (superfine) sugar

1 To make the dressing, place the egg yolks in a screw-top jar with the mustard, groundnut and walnut oils, lemon juice, parsley and sugar. Shake well to combine.

COOK'S TIP
The dressing for this salad uses raw egg yolks. Be sure to use only the freshest eggs from a reputable supplier. Pregnant women, young children and the elderly are advised not to eat raw egg yolks. This dressing can be made without the egg yolks if necessary.

2 Slice the mushrooms thinly with a sharp knife, keeping the slices intact if you can.

3 Transfer the sliced mushrooms to a large bowl and combine with the dressing. Set aside for 10–15 minutes to allow the flavours to mingle.

4 Meanwhile, preheat the grill (broiler) to medium-hot, place the walnut pieces in a grill (broiling) pan and toast for about a minute, shaking the pan to ensure they toast evenly. Alternatively, dry-fry them on a griddle.

5 Wash and spin the mixed salad leaves, then add to the mushrooms in the bowl and toss to combine.

6 To serve, spoon the salad on to four large plates, season well then scatter with the toasted walnuts and shavings of Parmesan cheese.

COOK'S TIP
If fresh ceps are unavailable, this salad can also be made with a range of other fresh mushrooms. Chestnut mushrooms, fresh shiitake mushrooms and even the familiar button (white) mushrooms would all work well.

VARIATION
For special occasions, two or three drops of truffle oil will impart a deep and mysterious flavour.

CHICKEN SALAD WITH HERBS AND LAVENDER

THE DELIGHTFUL SCENT OF LAVENDER HAS A NATURAL AFFINITY WITH SWEET GARLIC, THYME, MARJORAM AND ORANGE. THE ADDITION OF FRIED POLENTA OR CORN MEAL MAKES THIS SALAD BOTH FILLING AND DELICIOUS.

SERVES FOUR

INGREDIENTS
 4 boneless chicken breasts
 900ml/1½ pints/3¾ cups light
   chicken stock
 175g/6oz/1½ cups fine polenta
   or corn meal
 50g/2oz/¼ cup butter, plus extra
   for greasing
 450g/1lb young spinach
 175g/6oz lamb's lettuce
 8 small tomatoes, halved
 salt and ground black pepper
 8 sprigs fresh lavender, to garnish
For the marinade
 6 fresh lavender flowers
 10ml/2 tsp finely grated (shredded)
   orange rind
 2 garlic cloves, crushed
 10ml/2 tsp clear honey
 30ml/2 tbsp olive oil
 10ml/2 tsp chopped fresh thyme
 10ml/2 tsp chopped fresh marjoram
 salt

1 To make the marinade, strip the lavender flowers from the stems and combine with the orange rind, garlic, honey and salt. Add the oil and herbs.

2 Slash the chicken deeply, spread the mixture over and leave to marinate in the refrigerator for 20 minutes.

3 To make the polenta, bring the chicken stock to the boil in a heavy pan. Add the polenta or corn meal in a steady stream, stirring all the time until thick. Turn the cooked polenta or corn meal out on to a shallow, buttered tray and leave to cool.

COOK'S TIP
When preparing the spinach, tear the leaves into smaller pieces just before you are ready to serve. Do not cut them with a knife, as this tends to make the edges turn brown.

4 Cook the chicken on a medium barbecue or under the grill (broiler) for 15 minutes, basting with the marinade and turning once, until cooked through.

5 Cut the polenta into 2.5cm/1in cubes using a wet knife.

6 Heat the butter in a large frying pan and fry the polenta until it is golden.

7 Divide the spinach and lamb's lettuce among four dinner plates. Slice each chicken breast and arrange among the salad. Add the polenta and tomato halves to each plate.

8 Season each salad with salt and ground black pepper and garnish with sprigs of lavender. Serve immediately.

LITTLE ONIONS <u>WITH</u> CORIANDER, WINE <u>AND</u> OLIVE OIL

CHILLIES AND TOASTED CORIANDER SEEDS ADD PIQUANCY TO THE SMALL ONIONS USED HERE. BAY, GARLIC, THYME, OREGANO, LEMON AND PARSLEY PROVIDE AN UNMISTAKABLY MEDITERRANEAN KICK.

SERVES SIX

INGREDIENTS

105ml/7 tbsp olive oil
675g/1½lb small onions, peeled
150ml/¼ pint/⅔ cup dry white wine
2 bay leaves
2 garlic cloves, bruised
1–2 small dried red chillies
15ml/1 tbsp coriander seeds, toasted
  and lightly crushed
2.5ml/½ tsp sugar
a few fresh thyme sprigs
30ml/2 tbsp currants
10ml/2 tsp chopped fresh oregano
  or marjoram
5ml/1 tsp grated (shredded) lemon rind
15ml/1 tbsp chopped fresh flat
  leaf parsley
30–45ml/2–3 tbsp pine nuts, toasted
salt and ground black pepper

1 Place 30ml/2 tbsp of the olive oil in a wide pan. Add the onions, place over a medium heat and cook gently for about 5 minutes, or until the onions begin to colour. Use a draining spoon to remove from the pan and set aside.

2 Add the remaining oil, the wine, bay leaves, garlic, chillies, coriander seeds, sugar and thyme to the pan.

3 Bring to the boil and cook briskly for 5 minutes. Return the onions to the pan. Add the currants, reduce the heat and cook gently for 15–20 minutes, or until the onions are tender but not falling apart.

4 Use a draining spoon to transfer the onions to a serving dish, then boil the liquid vigorously until it reduces considerably. Taste and adjust the seasoning, if necessary, then pour the liquid over the onions.

5 Scatter the chopped oregano or marjoram over the onions in the dish, then cool and chill them.

6 Just before you are ready to serve the onions, stir in the grated lemon rind, chopped flat leaf parsley and toasted pine nuts.

COOK'S TIP
You might like to serve this dish as part of a mixed hors d'oeuvre – an antipasto – perhaps accompanied by mild mayonnaise-dressed celeriac salad and some thinly sliced prosciutto or other air-dried ham.

ROAST GARLIC <u>WITH</u> GOAT'S CHEESE, WALNUT <u>AND</u> HERB PÂTÉ

THE COMBINATION OF SWEET, MELLOW ROASTED GARLIC AND GOAT'S CHEESE IS A CLASSIC ONE. COOKING THE GARLIC WITH SPRIGS OF ROSEMARY AND THYME MAKES IT MORE AROMATIC. THE PÂTÉ IS PARTICULARLY GOOD MADE WITH FRESH THYME AND PARSLEY, AND THE NEW SEASON'S WALNUTS.

SERVES FOUR

INGREDIENTS
  4 large garlic bulbs
  4 fresh rosemary sprigs
  8 fresh thyme sprigs
  60ml/4 tbsp olive oil
  coarse salt and ground black pepper
For the pâté
  175g/6oz/¾ cup soft goat's cheese
  5ml/1 tsp finely chopped fresh thyme
  15ml/1 tbsp finely chopped
    fresh parsley
  50g/2oz/½ cup chopped
    shelled walnuts
  15ml/1 tbsp walnut oil (optional)
To serve
  4–8 slices sourdough bread
  shelled walnuts

1 Preheat the oven to 180°C/350°F/ Gas 4. Strip the papery outer skin from the garlic bulbs. Place them in an ovenproof dish large enough to hold them snugly.

2 Tuck the rosemary and thyme sprigs between the garlic bulbs, drizzle the oil over and season to taste with coarse salt and black pepper.

VARIATION
If you prefer, the pâté can also be made with other kinds of chopped nuts, such as hazelnuts and cashews.

3 Cover the garlic closely with foil and bake for 50–60 minutes, basting once. Leave to cool.

4 Preheat the grill (broiler). To make the pâté, cream the cheese with the thyme, parsley and chopped walnuts. Beat in 15ml/1 tbsp of the cooking oil from the garlic and season to taste, then transfer the pâté to a serving bowl.

5 Brush the sourdough bread with the remaining cooking oil from the garlic, then grill (broil) until toasted.

6 Drizzle the walnut oil, if using, over the pâté and grind some black pepper over it. Place a bulb of garlic on each plate and serve with the pâté and toasted bread. Serve with a few shelled walnuts and a little coarse salt.

VEGETABLES WITH TAPENADE AND HERB AIOLI

*THE DELICATE BUT DISTINCTIVE FLAVOURS OF CHERVIL, TARRAGON AND PARSLEY ARE COMBINED WITH
GARLIC FOR THIS HERB AIOLI. HERE, IT ACCOMPANIES A FULL-FLAVOURED TAPENADE AND IS SERVED
WITH A PLATTER OF SUMMER VEGETABLES AND QUAIL'S EGGS.*

SERVES SIX

INGREDIENTS
  2 red (bell) peppers, cut into
    wide strips
  30ml/2 tbsp olive oil
  225g/8oz new potatoes
  115g/4oz green beans
  225g/8oz baby carrots
  225g/8oz young asparagus
  12 quail's eggs
  fresh herbs, to garnish
  coarse salt, for sprinkling
For the tapenade
  175g/6oz/1½ cups pitted black olives
  50g/2oz can anchovy fillets, drained
  30ml/2 tbsp capers
  about 120ml/4fl oz/½ cup olive oil
  finely grated (shredded) rind of
    1 lemon
  15ml/1 tbsp brandy (optional)
For the herb aioli
  5 garlic cloves, crushed
  2 egg yolks
  5ml/1 tsp Dijon mustard
  about 10ml/2 tsp white wine vinegar
  250ml/8fl oz/1 cup light olive oil
  45ml/3 tbsp chopped mixed fresh
    herbs, such as chervil, parsley
    and tarragon
  30ml/2 tbsp chopped watercress
  salt and ground black pepper

1 To make the tapenade, finely chop
the olives, anchovies and capers and
beat together with the oil, lemon rind
and brandy, if using. (Alternatively,
lightly process the ingredients in a
blender or food processor.)

2 Season the tapenade with pepper
and blend in a little more oil if the
mixture seems very dry. Transfer to
a serving dish.

3 To make the aioli, beat together the
garlic, egg yolks, mustard and vinegar.
Gradually blend in the olive oil, a drop
at a time, whisking the mixture well
until thick and smooth.

4 Stir in the mixed herbs and chopped
watercress. Season with salt and pepper
to taste, adding a little more vinegar if
necessary. Cover with clear film and
chill until ready to serve.

5 Brush the peppers with oil, and place
on a hot barbecue or under a hot grill
(broiler) until they begin to char.

6 Cook the potatoes in a large pan of
boiling, salted water until tender. Add
the beans and carrots and blanch for
1 minute. Add the asparagus and cook
for a further 30 seconds. Drain the
vegetables. Cook the quail's eggs in
boiling water for 2 minutes.

7 Arrange all the vegetables, eggs and
sauces on a serving platter. Garnish
with fresh herbs and serve with coarse
salt, for sprinkling.

COOK'S TIPS
• Stir any leftover tapenade into pasta or
spread on to warm toast.
• If you are making this dish as part of
a picnic, allow the vegetables to cool
before packing in an airtight container.
Pack the quail's eggs in the original box.

fish, poultry & meat

Buy a fresh piece of fish, combine it with fragrant herbs and you

cannot go wrong. Fish has an affinity with many herbs, and the

choice of cooking methods and herb combinations are extensive.

Try richly flavoured, grilled red mullet or snapper with rosemary, or

tuna steaks with a deliciously peppery coriander crust. The same

diversity of choice applies equally to meat and poultry. Chicken

roasted with sage, thyme and lemon is absolutely delicious. So, too,

is a classic Languedoc Cassoulet, cooked long and slow with

beans, vegetables, garlic and parsley.

GRILLED COD FILLET <u>WITH</u> FRESH MIXED-HERB CRUST

DELICATELY FLAVOURED CHERVIL AND PARSLEY GO ESPECIALLY WELL WITH FISH. HERE, THEY ARE COMBINED WITH CHIVES AND WHOLEMEAL BREADCRUMBS TO MAKE A DELICIOUS CRUST FOR GRILLED OR BARBECUED COD.

SERVES FOUR

INGREDIENTS

25g/1oz/2 tbsp butter
4 thick pieces of cod fillet, about
  225g/8oz each, skinned
175g/6oz/3 cups wholemeal (whole-
  wheat) breadcrumbs
15ml/1 tbsp chopped fresh chervil
15ml/1 tbsp chopped fresh parsley,
  plus extra sprigs to garnish
15ml/1 tbsp chopped fresh chives
15ml/1 tbsp olive oil
salt and ground black pepper
lemon wedges, to garnish

1 Melt the butter and brush over the cod fillets. Mix any remaining butter with the breadcrumbs, fresh herbs and plenty of salt and ground black pepper.

2 Cook the fish under a medium grill (broiler) for about 10 minutes, turning once. Increase the heat, then press a quarter of the crust mixture on to each fillet, spreading evenly to cover. Lightly sprinkle olive oil over the top and cook for a further 2 minutes, or until the topping is golden brown.

3 Serve the fish garnished with lemon wedges and the sprigs of fresh parsley.

VARIATION
This mixed-herb crust works well with any firm white fish.

GRILLED RED MULLET WITH ROSEMARY

THIS RECIPE IS VERY SIMPLE — THE TASTE OF GRILLED RED MULLET IS SO GOOD IN ITSELF THAT IT NEEDS VERY LITTLE TO BRING OUT THE FLAVOUR: GARLIC AND JUST A HINT OF ROSEMARY ARE ALL THAT ARE NEEDED.

SERVES FOUR

INGREDIENTS
  4 red mullet or snapper, about
    275g/10oz each, cleaned
  4 garlic cloves, cut lengthways into
    thin slivers
  75ml/5 tbsp olive oil
  30ml/2 tbsp balsamic vinegar
  10ml/2 tsp very finely chopped fresh
    rosemary or 5ml/1 tsp dried
  ground black pepper
  fresh rosemary sprigs and lemon
    wedges, to garnish
  coarse salt, to serve

COOK'S TIP
Red mullet are extra delicious cooked on the barbecue. If possible, enclose them in a basket grill so that they are easy to turn over.

1 Cut three diagonal slits in both sides of each fish with a sharp kitchen knife. Push the garlic slivers into the slits in the fish.

2 Place the fish in a single layer in a shallow dish. Make a marinade by whisking the olive oil, balsamic vinegar and rosemary with ground black pepper to taste.

3 Pour the liquid over the fish, cover with clear film and leave to marinate in the refrigerator for at least 1 hour. Grill (broil) for 5–6 minutes on each side, turning once and brushing with the marinade.

4 Serve hot, sprinkled with coarse salt and garnished with fresh rosemary sprigs and lemon wedges.

SALMON WITH SUMMER HERB MARINADE

MAKE THE BEST USE OF SUMMER HERBS IN THIS MARINADE. TRY ANY COMBINATION OF HERBS, DEPENDING ON WHAT YOU HAVE TO HAND. SALMON IS PERFECT, BUT THE MARINADE CAN ALSO BE USED WITH OTHER FISH, MEAT AND POULTRY.

SERVES FOUR

INGREDIENTS

large handful of fresh herb sprigs,
  such as chervil, thyme, parsley,
  sage, chives, rosemary, oregano
90ml/6 tbsp olive oil
45ml/3 tbsp tarragon vinegar
1 garlic clove, crushed
2 spring onions (scallions), chopped
4 salmon steaks or thick fillets
salt and ground black pepper
salad leaves and lemon wedges,
  to serve

1 Discard any coarse stalks or damaged leaves from the herbs, then chop them very finely.

2 Put the chopped herbs into a large bowl and add the oil, tarragon vinegar, garlic and chopped spring onions. Stir to mix thoroughly.

3 Place the salmon in a bowl and pour over the marinade. Cover and leave to marinate in a cool place for 4–6 hours.

4 Drain the salmon. Cook under a medium grill (broiler) for 10–15 minutes, turning once. Use the marinade to baste the fish occasionally.

5 The fish is cooked when the flesh separates into flakes when it is gently lifted with a knife. Serve with salad leaves and lemon wedges.

HALIBUT FILLETS WITH FRESH TOMATO AND BASIL SALSA

A FRESH-TASTING TOMATO SALSA ENLIVENED WITH JALAPEÑO PEPPER AND BASIL IS IDEAL WITH SIMPLY GRILLED OR BARBECUED HALIBUT.

SERVES FOUR

INGREDIENTS

    4 halibut fillets, about 175g/
      6oz each
    45ml/3 tbsp olive oil
    basil leaves, to garnish
For the salsa
    1 tomato, roughly chopped
    ¼ red onion, finely sliced
    1 small jalapeño pepper, chopped
    30ml/2 tbsp balsamic vinegar
    10 large fresh basil leaves
    15ml/1 tbsp olive oil
    salt and ground black pepper

1 To make the salsa, mix together the chopped tomato, red onion, jalapeño pepper and balsamic vinegar in a bowl. Slice the fresh basil leaves finely, using a sharp kitchen knife.

2 Stir the basil and the olive oil into the tomato mixture. Season to taste. Cover the bowl with clear film and leave to marinate for at least 3 hours.

3 Rub the halibut fillets with oil, and season. Cook under a medium grill (broiler), or on a barbecue, for 8 minutes, basting with oil and turning once. Garnish with basil and serve with the salsa.

COOK'S TIP

It is easy to overcook halibut, which will make it turn dry and spoil its excellent flavour.

PAN-FRIED COD <u>WITH</u> CREAMY VERMOUTH <u>AND</u> HERB SAUCE

CHUNKY COD IS TEAMED WITH A QUICK PAN SAUCE OF VERMOUTH, CREAMY GOAT'S CHEESE, PARSLEY AND CHERVIL. GRILLED PLUM TOMATOES MAKE THE PERFECT ACCOMPANIMENT.

2 Heat a non-stick frying pan, then add 15ml/1 tbsp of the oil, swirling it around to coat the bottom. Add the pieces of cod and cook, without turning or moving them, for 4 minutes, or until nicely caramelized.

3 Turn each piece over and cook the other side for a further 3 minutes, or until just firm. Remove it to a serving plate and keep hot.

4 Heat the remaining oil and stir-fry the spring onions for 1 minute. Add the vermouth and cook until reduced by half. Add the stock and cook again until reduced by half.

SERVES FOUR

INGREDIENTS
    4 pieces of cod fillet, about
      150g/5oz each, skinned
    30ml/2 tbsp olive oil
    4 spring onions (scallions), chopped
    150ml/¼ pint/⅔ cup dry vermouth,
      preferably Noilly Prat
    300ml/½ pint/1¼ cups fish stock
    45ml/3 tbsp crème fraîche or
      double (heavy) cream
    65g/2½oz goat's cheese, rind
      removed, and chopped
    30ml/2 tbsp chopped fresh parsley
    15ml/1 tbsp chopped fresh chervil
    salt and ground black pepper
    flat leaf parsley, to garnish
    grilled plum tomatoes, to serve

1 Remove any stray bones from the cod fillets. Rinse the fish under cold running water and pat dry with kitchen paper. Place on a plate and season well.

COOK'S TIP
The cooking time may change according to the thickness of the fish fillets.

5 Stir in the crème fraîche or cream and goat's cheese and simmer for 3 minutes. Add salt and pepper, stir in the herbs and spoon over the fish. Garnish with parsley and serve with grilled tomatoes.

VARIATION
Instead of cod you could use salmon, haddock or plaice.

PAN-FRIED SALMON <u>WITH</u> TARRAGON <u>AND</u> MUSHROOM SAUCE

TARRAGON HAS A DISTINCTIVE ANISEED FLAVOUR THAT IS GOOD WITH FISH, CRÈME FRAÎCHE AND MUSHROOMS. OYSTER MUSHROOMS HAVE BEEN INCLUDED HERE TO PROVIDE TEXTURE AND FLAVOUR.

SERVES FOUR

INGREDIENTS
  50g/2oz/¼ cup unsalted (sweet)
    butter
  4 salmon steaks, about 175g/6oz each
  1 shallot, finely chopped
  175g/6oz/2½ cups assorted wild and
    cultivated mushrooms such as
    oyster mushrooms, saffron milk-
    caps, bay boletus or cauliflower
    fungus, trimmed and sliced
  200ml/7fl oz/scant 1 cup chicken or
    vegetable stock
  10ml/2 tsp cornflour (cornstarch)
  2.5ml/½ tsp mustard
  50ml/3½ tbsp crème fraîche
  45ml/3 tbsp chopped fresh tarragon
  5ml/1 tsp white wine vinegar
  salt and cayenne pepper
  new potatoes and a green salad,
    to serve

1 Melt half of the butter in a large, non-stick frying pan, season the salmon and cook in batches over a moderate heat for 8 minutes, turning once. Transfer to a plate, cover and keep warm.

COOK'S TIP
Fresh tarragon will bruise and darken quickly after chopping, so prepare the herb just before you use it.

2 Heat the remaining butter in the pan and gently fry the shallot to soften without letting it colour. Add the mushrooms and cook until the juices begin to flow. Add the stock and simmer for 2–3 minutes.

3 Put the cornflour and mustard in a cup and blend with 15ml/1 tbsp water. Stir into the mushroom mixture and bring to a simmer, stirring, to thicken. Add the crème fraîche, tarragon, vinegar, and salt and pepper.

4 Spoon the mushrooms over each salmon steak and serve with new potatoes and a green salad.

FILLETS OF HAKE BAKED WITH THYME AND GARLIC

QUICK COOKING IS THE ESSENCE OF THIS SIMPLE DISH. GARLIC, LEMON AND A HINT OF THYME ARE ALL THAT ARE NEEDED TO ENHANCE THE FLAVOUR OF THE HAKE.

SERVES FOUR

INGREDIENTS

4 hake fillets, about 175g/6oz each
1 shallot, finely chopped
2 garlic cloves, thinly sliced
4 sprigs fresh thyme, plus extra
  to garnish
grated (shredded) rind and juice
  of 1 lemon
30ml/2 tbsp extra virgin olive oil
salt and ground black pepper

1 Preheat the oven to 180ºC/350ºF/ Gas 4. Lay the hake fillets in the base of a large roasting tin (pan). Scatter the shallot, garlic and thyme on top.

2 Season the fish well with salt and ground black pepper.

VARIATION
If hake is not available, you can use cod or haddock fillets for this recipe.

3 Drizzle the lemon juice and olive oil over the fish. Bake in the preheated oven for about 15 minutes. Serve immediately, scattered with finely grated lemon rind and garnished with the extra thyme sprigs.

BAKED TUNA <u>WITH A</u> CORIANDER CRUST

FRESH TUNA IS VERY MEATY AND FILLING AND IS EXCELLENT ACCOMPANIED BY A LIGHT SALSA OF MANGO AND LIME WITH JUST A DASH OF CHILLI. TOPPING THE FISH WITH A FRESH CORIANDER AND LEMON CRUST ADDS A TASTY CRISPNESS.

SERVES FOUR

INGREDIENTS
   finely grated rind of 1 lemon
   5ml/1 tsp black peppercorns
   ½ small onion, finely chopped
   30ml/2 tbsp chopped fresh
     coriander (cilantro)
   4 fresh tuna steaks, about 175g/
     6oz each
   120ml/4fl oz/½ cup olive oil
For the salsa
   1 mango, peeled, stone removed and
     cut into dice
   finely grated (shredded) rind and
     juice of 1 lime
   ½ red chilli, deseeded and chopped

2 Mix together the lemon rind, black peppercorns, chopped onion and fresh coriander in a mortar and pestle to make a coarse paste.

3 Spread the paste on to one side of each tuna steak, pressing on well to ensure it sticks.

4 Heat the olive oil in a heavy frying pan until it begins to smoke. Add the tuna, paste-side down, and fry until a crust forms. Lower the heat and turn the steaks to cook for 1 minute more.

5 Pat off any excess oil on to absorbent kitchen paper, and serve with the mango salsa.

1 To make the mango salsa, mix the mango, lime rind and juice, and chilli in a bowl and leave to marinate for at least 1 hour.

ROAST MONKFISH WITH GARLIC AND BAY LEAVES

MONKFISH QUICKLY ROASTED WITH GARLIC AND BAY IS DELICIOUS SERVED WITH NEW POTATOES FOR A SUMMERTIME MEAL.

SERVES SIX

INGREDIENTS

1.2kg/2½lb monkfish tail
8 garlic cloves
15ml/1 tbsp olive oil
2 fennel bulbs, sliced
juice and grated (shredded) rind of
   1 lemon
2 bay leaves, plus extra to garnish
salt and ground black pepper

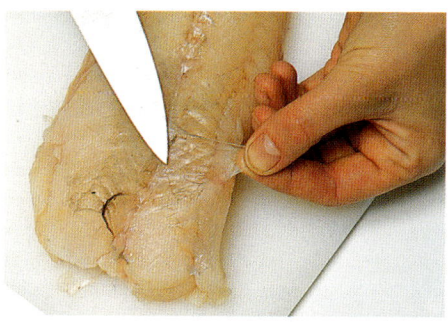

1 Preheat the oven to 220°C/425°F/ Gas 7. With a sharp filleting knife, carefully cut away the thin membrane covering the outside of the monkfish; keep the knife flat against the fish to avoid cutting too much of the flesh away. When finished, discard the membrane.

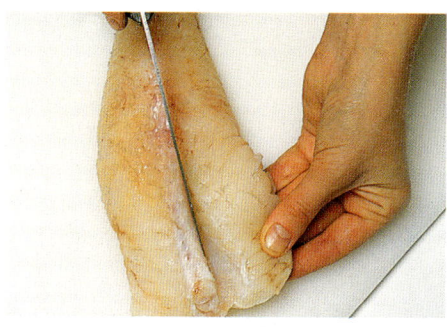

2 Cut along one side of the central bone to remove the fillet. Repeat on the other side. Discard the bone.

VARIATION
Monkfish is usually available all the year round, but if it is not available then you could substitute another firm white fish.

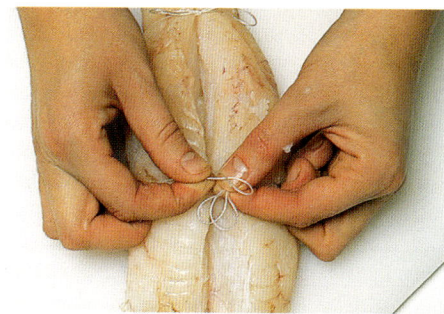

3 Tie the separated fillets together with string to reshape as a tailpiece.

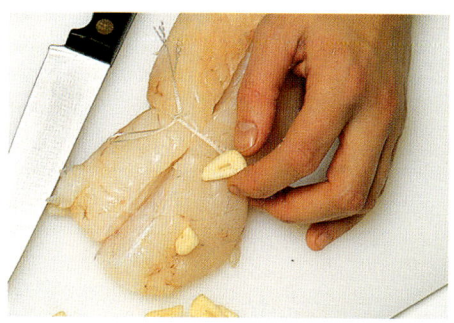

4 Peel and slice the garlic cloves and cut incisions into the fish flesh. Place the garlic slices in the incisions.

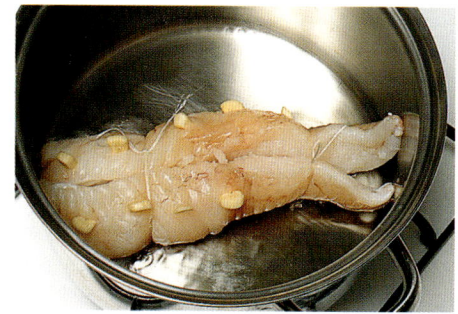

5 Heat the oil in a large, heavy pan and cook the fish until sealed on all sides, then place in a roasting pan together with the fennel slices, lemon juice, bay leaves and seasoning.

6 Roast the fish in the oven for about 20 minutes, until tender and cooked through. Serve immediately, garnished with bay leaves and lemon rind.

BAKED CHICKEN WITH SHALLOTS, GARLIC AND FENNEL

THIS IS A VERY SIMPLE AND DELICIOUS WAY TO COOK CHICKEN. LEAVE THE CHICKEN TO MARINATE FOR A FEW HOURS BEFORE BAKING SO THAT THE COMPLEMENTARY FLAVOURS OF GARLIC, SHALLOTS AND FENNEL SEEDS CAN REALLY PERMEATE THE FLESH.

SERVES FOUR

INGREDIENTS

1.6–1.8kg/3½–4lb chicken, cut into
  8 pieces or 8 chicken joints
250g/9oz shallots, chopped
1 head garlic, separated into cloves
  and peeled
60ml/4 tbsp extra virgin olive oil
45ml/3 tbsp tarragon vinegar
45ml/3 tbsp white wine or
  vermouth (optional)
5ml/1 tsp fennel seeds,
  lightly crushed
2 bulbs fennel, cut into wedges,
  feathery tops reserved
150ml/¼ pint/⅔ cup double
  (heavy) cream
5ml/1 tsp redcurrant jelly
15ml/1 tbsp tarragon mustard
caster (superfine) sugar (optional)
30ml/2 tbsp chopped fresh flat
  leaf parsley
salt and ground black pepper

1 Place the chicken, shallots and all but one of the garlic cloves in a flameproof dish or roasting pan. Add the oil, vinegar, wine or vermouth, if using, and fennel seeds. Season with pepper and mix well, then marinate for 2–3 hours.

2 Preheat the oven to 190°C/375°F/ Gas 5. Add the fennel to the chicken, season with salt, and stir to mix. Cook for 50–60 minutes, stirring once or twice. The juices should run clear when the thigh is pierced with a skewer.

3 Transfer the chicken and vegetables to a serving dish and keep warm. Skim off some of the fat and bring the juices to the boil, then pour in the cream. Stir, then whisk in the redcurrant jelly and mustard. Check the seasoning, adding a little sugar, if you like.

4 Chop the remaining garlic with the reserved fennel tops and mix with the chopped parsley. Pour the sauce over the chicken and scatter the chopped garlic and herb mixture over the top. Serve immediately.

COOK'S TIPS
• If possible, use the fresh new season's garlic for this dish, as it is plump, moist and full of flavour. Purple-skinned garlic is considered to have the best flavour.
• The cut surfaces of fennel tend to discolour quickly, so try not to prepare it much in advance of using it. If you must, then put the wedges into a bowl of cold water that has been acidulated with a little lemon juice.

LAVENDER AND THYME CHICKEN

HERE, LAVENDER FLOWERS ARE USED TO PERFUME AND FLAVOUR CHICKEN COOKED IN A LARGE CASSEROLE WITH RED WINE, ORANGE AND THYME. WHEN THE LID IS REMOVED AFTER COOKING, THE HEADY AROMA WILL ENTICE AS MUCH AS THE DELICIOUS FLAVOUR.

SERVES FOUR

INGREDIENTS
  4 chicken portions
  15ml/1 tbsp butter
  15ml/1 tbsp olive oil
  8 shallots
  30ml/2 tbsp plain (all-purpose) flour
  250ml/8fl oz/1 cup red wine
  250ml/8fl oz/1 cup chicken stock
  4 sprigs thyme
  10ml/2 tsp thyme flowers, removed
    from the stalk
  10ml/2 tsp lavender flowers
  grated (shredded) rind and juice of
    1 orange
  salt and ground black pepper
For the garnish
  1 orange, divided into segments
  12 lavender sprigs
  20ml/4 tsp lavender flowers

1 Cut each chicken portion into two using a large, sharp knife.

2 Heat the butter and olive oil in a heavy pan and add the chicken pieces. Cook them for about 5 minutes, or until they are browned all over, then transfer to a large, flameproof casserole.

3 Add the shallots to the frying pan and cook for 2 minutes. Add to the chicken in the casserole.

4 Add the flour to the frying pan, and cook for 2 minutes, stirring continuously. Pour in enough of the wine and stock to make a thin sauce. Bring to the boil, stirring all the time, and season to taste.

5 Stir in the thyme sprigs, thyme and lavender flowers, orange rind and juice.

6 Pour the sauce over the chicken in the casserole, then cover and simmer for 30–40 minutes, or until the chicken is tender.

7 Remove the thyme sprigs before serving. Serve the stew garnished with orange segments, and fresh lavender sprigs and flowers.

CHICKEN WITH FRESH HERBS AND GARLIC

THYME, SAGE, GARLIC AND LEMON COMBINE TO GIVE ROAST CHICKEN A SUMMERY FLAVOUR.
IF YOU PREFER, COOK THE CHICKEN ON A SPIT ON THE BARBECUE.

SERVES FOUR

INGREDIENTS

2kg/4½lb free-range chicken
finely grated (shredded) rind and
  juice of 1 lemon
1 garlic clove, crushed
30ml/2 tbsp olive oil
2 fresh thyme sprigs
2 fresh sage sprigs
90ml/6 tbsp unsalted (sweet) butter,
  softened
salt and ground black pepper

COOK'S TIP
If you are roasting a chicken to serve
cold, cooking it in foil helps to keep it
succulent – open the foil for the last
20 minutes to brown the skin, then close
it as the chicken cools.

1 Season the chicken well and place in
a shallow non-metallic dish.

2 Mix the lemon rind and juice, crushed
garlic and olive oil together and pour
them over the chicken. Leave to
marinate in the refrigerator for at least
2 hours. Preheat the oven to 230ºC/
450ºF/Gas 8.

3 Place the herbs in the cavity of the
bird and smear the butter over the skin.
Roast in the oven for 1½–1¾ hours,
reducing the heat to 190ºC/375ºF/Gas 5
after the first 10 minutes. Baste with
marinade during cooking. The chicken
is cooked when the juices run clear
when the thigh is pierced with a skewer.
Leave for 15 minutes before carving.

CHICKEN WITH TARRAGON CREAM

THE ANISEED-LIKE FLAVOUR OF TARRAGON HAS A PARTICULAR AFFINITY WITH CHICKEN, ESPECIALLY IN CREAMY SAUCES SUCH AS THE ONE IN THIS FAVOURITE FRENCH BISTRO-STYLE DISH. SERVE SEASONAL VEGETABLES AND BOILED RED CAMARGUE RICE WITH THE CHICKEN.

SERVES FOUR

INGREDIENTS

30ml/2 tbsp light olive oil
4 chicken supremes, each weighing about 250g/9oz
3 shallots, finely chopped
2 garlic cloves, finely chopped
115g/4oz/1½ cups wild mushrooms or shiitake mushrooms, halved
150ml/¼ pint/⅔ cup dry white wine
300ml/½ pint/1¼ cups double (heavy) cream
15g/½oz mixed fresh tarragon and flat leaf parsley, chopped
salt and ground black pepper
sprigs of fresh tarragon and flat leaf parsley, to garnish

COOK'S TIP

Chicken fillets could be used in place of the chicken supremes.

1 Heat the light olive oil in a large frying pan and add the chicken supremes, skin-side down. Cook for 10 minutes, turning the chicken twice, or until it is a golden brown colour on both sides.

2 Reduce the heat and cook the chicken breasts for 10 minutes more, turning occasionally. Use a slotted spoon to remove the chicken breasts from the pan and set aside.

3 Add the shallots and garlic to the pan and cook gently, stirring, until the shallots are softened but not browned. Increase the heat, add the mushrooms and stir-fry for 2 minutes, or until the mushrooms just start to colour.

4 Replace the chicken, nesting the pieces down into the other ingredients, and then pour in the wine. Simmer for 5–10 minutes, or until most of the wine has evaporated.

5 Add the cream and gently move the ingredients around in the pan to mix in the cream. Simmer for 10 minutes, or until the sauce has thickened. Stir the chopped herbs into the sauce with seasoning to taste. Arrange the chicken on warm plates and spoon the sauce over. Garnish with sprigs of tarragon and flat leaf parsley.

SPATCHCOCK POUSSINS <u>WITH</u> HERBES DE PROVENCE BUTTER

SPATCHCOCK IS SAID TO BE A DISTORTION OF AN 18TH CENTURY IRISH EXPRESSION "DISPATCH COCK" FOR PROVIDING AN UNEXPECTED GUEST WITH A QUICK AND SIMPLE MEAL. A YOUNG CHICKEN WAS PREPARED WITHOUT FRILLS OR FUSS BY BEING SPLIT, FLATTENED AND FRIED OR GRILLED.

SERVES FOUR

INGREDIENTS

2 poussins, each weighing
   about 450g/1lb
1 shallot, finely chopped
2 garlic cloves, crushed
45ml/3 tbsp chopped mixed fresh
   herbs, such as flat leaf parsley,
   sage, rosemary and thyme
75g/3oz/6 tbsp butter, softened
salt and ground black pepper

VARIATIONS
Add some finely chopped chilli or a little grated lemon rind to the butter.

1 To spatchcock a poussin, place it breast down on a chopping board and split it along the back. Open out the bird and turn it over, so that the breast side is uppermost. Press the bird as flat as possible, then thread two metal skewers through it, across the breast and thigh, to keep it flat. Repeat with the second poussin and place the skewered birds on a grill (broiler) pan.

2 Add the chopped shallot, crushed garlic and chopped mixed herbs to the butter with plenty of seasoning, and then beat well. Dot the butter over the spatchcock poussins.

3 Preheat the grill to high and cook the poussins for 30 minutes, turning them over halfway through. Turn again and baste with the cooking juices, then cook for a further 5–7 minutes on each side.

LEMON GRASS PORK CHOPS
WITH MUSHROOMS

THAI FLAVOURINGS WITH LEMON GRASS, CHILLI AND SPRING ONIONS ARE USED TO MAKE AN AROMATIC MARINADE AND A SPICY SAUCE FOR GRILLED OR BARBECUED PORK. THE SAUCE CAN BE PUT TOGETHER IN A PAN ON THE BARBECUE WHILE THE CHOPS AND MUSHROOMS ARE COOKING.

SERVES FOUR

INGREDIENTS

4 pork chops, about 225g/8oz each
4 large field (portabello) mushrooms
45ml/3 tbsp vegetable oil
4 fresh red chillies, seeded and
  finely sliced
45ml/3 tbsp Thai fish sauce (*nam pla*)
90ml/6 tbsp lime juice
4 shallots, chopped
5ml/1 tsp roasted ground rice
30ml/2 tbsp spring onions
  (scallions), chopped
fresh coriander (cilantro) leaves and
  4 spring onions (scallions) sliced
  lengthways, to garnish
For the marinade
2 garlic cloves, chopped
15ml/1 tbsp sugar
15ml/1 tbsp Thai fish sauce (*nam pla*)
30ml/2 tbsp soy sauce
15ml/1 tbsp sesame oil
15ml/1 tbsp whisky or dry sherry
2 lemon grass stalks, finely chopped
2 spring onions (scallions), chopped

1 To make the marinade, mix all the ingredients together. Arrange the pork chops in a shallow dish. Pour over the marinade and leave for 1–2 hours.

COOK'S TIP
Thai fish sauce, or *nam pla*, is actually anchovy essence (paste). It has a clean, salty taste and enhances other flavours rather than swamping them.

2 Place the mushrooms and marinated pork chops on a grill rack (broiler), and brush with 15ml/1 tbsp vegetable oil.

3 Cook the pork chops under a medium-hot grill, or on a barbecue, for 10–15 minutes and the mushrooms for 2 minutes, turning once. Brush both with the marinade while cooking.

4 Meanwhile, heat the remaining oil in a small frying pan, then remove from the heat and mix in the remaining ingredients except the garnishes.

5 Put the pork chops and mushrooms on a serving plate and spoon over the sauce. Garnish with the fresh coriander and spring onions.

RABBIT AND LEMON GRASS RISOTTO

SCENTED LEMON GRASS IMPARTS A PLEASANT TANG TO THIS CREAMY RISOTTO. QUICKLY COOKED STRIPS OF TENDER RABBIT ADD A RICH FLAVOUR, WHILE FRESH THYME CONTRIBUTES FLAVOUR.

SERVES THREE TO FOUR

INGREDIENTS
    225g/8oz rabbit meat, cut into strips
    seasoned flour
    50g/2oz/¼ cup butter
    15ml/1 tbsp olive oil
    45ml/3 tbsp dry sherry
    1 onion, finely chopped
    1 garlic clove, crushed
    1 lemon grass stalk, peeled and very
        finely sliced
    275g/10oz/1½ cups risotto rice,
        preferably carnaroli
    1 litre/1¾ pints/4 cups simmering
        chicken stock
    10ml/2 tsp chopped fresh thyme
    45ml/3 tbsp double (heavy) cream
    25g/1oz/⅓ cup freshly grated
        (shredded) Parmesan cheese
    salt and ground black pepper

VARIATION
This recipe would also work well using chicken or turkey instead of the rabbit.

1 Coat the rabbit strips in the seasoned flour. Heat half the butter and olive oil in a frying pan and fry the rabbit quickly until evenly brown. Add the sherry, and allow to boil briefly to burn off the alcohol. Season with salt and pepper and set aside.

2 Heat the remaining olive oil and butter in a large pan. Fry the onion and garlic over a low heat for 4–5 minutes, or until the onion is soft. Add the sliced lemon grass and cook for a few more minutes.

3 Add the rice and stir to coat in the oil. Add a ladleful of stock and cook, stirring, until the liquid has been absorbed. Continue adding the stock gradually, stirring constantly. When the rice is almost cooked, stir in three-quarters of the meat, with the pan juices. Add the thyme and seasoning.

4 Continue cooking until the rice is tender but still has a "bite". Stir in the cream and Parmesan, remove from the heat and cover. Leave to rest before serving, garnished with rabbit strips.

LAMB STEAKS WITH MINT AND LEMON

USE THIS SIMPLE AND TRADITIONAL MARINADE TO MAKE THE MOST OF FINE-QUALITY LAMB LEG STEAKS. THE COMBINATION OF LEMON AND FRESH MINT GOES EXTREMELY WELL WITH THE FLAVOUR OF GRILLED OR BARBECUED LAMB.

SERVES FOUR

INGREDIENTS

    4 lamb steaks, about 225g/8oz each
    5ml/1 tsp finely chopped fresh mint
    fresh mint leaves, to garnish
For the marinade
    grated (shredded) rind and juice of
    ½ lemon
    1 garlic clove, crushed
    1 spring onion (scallion), finely chopped
    30ml/2 tbsp extra virgin olive oil
    salt and ground black pepper

1 Mix all the ingredients for the marinade and season to taste with salt and ground black pepper.

2 Place the lamb steaks in a shallow dish and add the marinade and mint, ensuring that all the meat is coated. Cover with clear film and leave the lamb to marinate in the refrigerator for several hours or overnight if possible.

3 Drain the lamb and cook under a medium-hot grill (broiler), or on a barbecue, for 10–15 minutes, or until just cooked, basting with marinade occasionally and turning once. Garnish with the fresh mint leaves.

CASSOULET DE LANGUEDOC

THERE ARE MANY REGIONAL VARIATIONS OF THIS CLASSIC FRENCH CASSEROLE OF SAUSAGE, BEANS AND ASSORTED MEATS, EACH WIDELY DIFFERENT FROM THE NEXT ACCORDING TO ITS TOWN OF ORIGIN. THE SLOW-COOKING METHOD ENSURES THE HERBS ADD A RICH DEPTH OF FLAVOUR.

SERVES EIGHT

INGREDIENTS
225g/8oz/1¼ cups dried haricot
   (navy) beans, soaked for 24 hours
2 large onions, 1 cut into chunks and
   1 chopped
1 large carrot, quartered
2 cloves
small handful of parsley stalks
225g/8oz lean gammon (smoked or
   cured ham), in one piece
4 duck leg quarters, split into thighs
   and drumsticks
225g/8oz lean lamb, trimmed
   and cubed
2 garlic cloves, finely chopped
75ml/5 tbsp dry white wine
175g/6oz cooked Toulouse sausage,
   or garlic sausage, skinned and
   coarsely chopped
400g/14oz can chopped tomatoes
salt and ground black pepper
For the topping
75g/3oz/1½ cups fresh white
   breadcrumbs
30ml/2 tbsp chopped fresh parsley
2 garlic cloves, finely chopped

1 Drain and thoroughly rinse the beans, then place them in a large pan and add the onion cut into chunks, carrot, cloves and parsley stalks. Pour in enough cold water to cover the beans completely and bring to the boil.

2 Boil the beans for 10 minutes, then reduce the heat, cover and simmer for 1½ hours, or until the beans are tender. Skim off any scum that rises to the surface and top up with boiling water as necessary. Drain the cooked beans, reserving the stock; discard the onion, carrot, cloves and parsley stalks.

3 Put the gammon into a pan and cover with cold water. Bring to the boil, reduce the heat and simmer for 10 minutes. Preheat the oven to150°C/300°F/Gas 2.

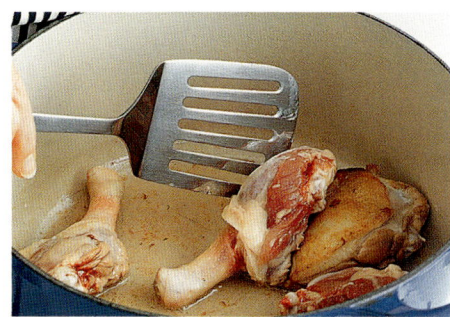

4 Heat a large, flameproof casserole and cook the duck portions in batches until golden brown on all sides. Use a slotted spoon to remove the duck portions from the casserole, set aside. Add and brown the lamb in batches, removing each batch and setting aside.

5 Pour off the excess fat from the casserole, leaving about 30ml/2 tbsp. Cook the onion and garlic in this fat. Stir in the wine. Remove from the heat.

6 Spoon a layer of beans into the casserole. Add the duck, lamb, gammon, sausage, tomatoes and more beans. Season each layer as you add them. Pour in enough of the reserved stock to cover the ingredients. Cover, and cook in the oven for 2½ hours. Check occasionally to ensure the beans are covered, add more stock if necessary.

7 Mix together the topping ingredients and sprinkle over the cassoulet. Cook, uncovered, for a further 30 minutes.

CHORIZO WITH GARLIC POTATOES

A CLASSIC TAPAS RECIPE, THIS SIMPLE DISH CAN BE SERVED IN SMALL QUANTITIES AS A SNACK OR, AS HERE, IN SLIGHTLY LARGER PROPORTIONS.

SERVES FOUR

INGREDIENTS

   450g/1lb potatoes, peeled
   3 eggs, hard-boiled and quartered
   175g/6oz chorizo sausage, sliced
   150ml/¼ pint/⅔ cup mayonnaise
   150ml/¼ pint/⅔ cup sour cream
   2 garlic cloves, crushed
   salt and ground black pepper
   30ml/2 tbsp chopped fresh coriander
      (cilantro), to garnish

VARIATION

To give this dish a more piquant flavour, add about 15ml/1 tbsp finely chopped cornichons and 4 finely chopped anchovy fillets. If coriander isn't available, then use 15ml/1 tbsp fresh marjoram instead.

1 Cook the potatoes in a pan of boiling salted water for 20 minutes, or until tender. Drain and leave to cool.

2 Cut the potatoes into bitesize pieces. Place them in a large serving dish with the eggs and chorizo sausage, and season to taste with salt and pepper.

3 In a small bowl, stir the mayonnaise, sour cream and garlic together with seasoning to taste, then spoon this dressing over the potato mixture.

4 Toss the salad gently to coat the ingredients with dressing, then sprinkle with chopped coriander to garnish.

vegetarian

Aromas such as garlic, lemon grass, lime, cardamom and ginger are vitally important in good vegetarian cooking. Freshly chopped herbs are perfect when added to mouthwatering combinations of fresh vegetables, cheese, nuts or pulses. Mix them into creamy risottos, a herb and spice paste for exotic curries, richly flavoured pasta sauces, crumbly crust bakes and stuffings for vegetables. You can't be too generous with the amount of herbs you throw in; vegetarian cooking is a great opportunity to show off their wealth of flavour and colour.

RISOTTO WITH BASIL AND RICOTTA

THIS IS A WELL-FLAVOURED RISOTTO, WHICH BENEFITS FROM THE DISTINCTIVE PUNGENCY OF BASIL, MELLOWED WITH SMOOTH RICOTTA.

SERVES THREE TO FOUR

INGREDIENTS
    45ml/3 tbsp olive oil
    1 onion, finely chopped
    275g/10oz/1½ cups risotto rice
    1 litre/1¾ pints/4 cups simmering
        vegetable stock
    175g/6oz/¾ cup ricotta cheese
    50g/2oz/generous 1 cup finely
        chopped fresh basil leaves, plus
        extra leaves to garnish
    75g/3oz/1 cup freshly grated
        (shredded) Parmesan cheese
    salt and ground black pepper

1 Heat the oil in a large pan or flameproof casserole and fry the chopped onion over a gentle heat, stirring frequently until it is soft.

2 Tip in the rice. Cook for a few minutes, stirring, until the rice is coated with oil and is slightly translucent.

3 Pour in about a quarter of the stock. Cook, stirring, until all the stock has been absorbed, then add another ladleful. Continue in this manner, adding more stock when the previous ladleful has been absorbed, for about 20 minutes, or until the rice is just tender.

4 Spoon the ricotta cheese into a bowl and break it up a little with a fork. Stir into the risotto along with the basil and Parmesan. Taste and adjust the seasoning, then cover and allow to stand for 2–3 minutes before serving, garnished with basil leaves.

ROSEMARY RISOTTO WITH BORLOTTI BEANS

THIS IS A CLASSIC RISOTTO WITH A SUBTLE AND COMPLEX TASTE, FROM THE HEADY FLAVOURS OF ROSEMARY TO THE SAVOURY BEANS AND THE FRUITY-SWEET TASTES OF MASCARPONE AND PARMESAN.

SERVES THREE TO FOUR

INGREDIENTS
   400g/14oz can borlotti beans
   30ml/2 tbsp olive oil
   1 onion, chopped
   2 garlic cloves, crushed
   275g/10oz/1½ cups risotto rice
   175ml/6fl oz/¾ cup dry white wine
   900ml–1 litre/1½–1¾ pints/
      3¾–4 cups simmering
      vegetable stock
   60ml/4 tbsp mascarpone cheese
   65g/2½oz/¾ cup freshly grated
      (shredded) Parmesan cheese,
      plus extra to serve (optional)
   5ml/1 tsp chopped fresh rosemary
   salt and ground black pepper

1 Drain the canned borlotti beans, rinse them well under plenty of cold water and drain again.

2 Purée about two-thirds of the beans fairly coarsely in a food processor or blender. Set the remainder aside.

3 Heat the olive oil in a large pan and gently fry the onion and garlic for 6–8 minutes, or until very soft. Add the rice and cook over a medium heat for a few minutes, stirring constantly, until the grains are thoroughly coated in oil and are slightly translucent.

4 Pour in the wine. Cook over a medium heat for 2–3 minutes, stirring all the time, until the wine has been absorbed. Add the stock gradually, a ladleful at a time, waiting for each quantity to be absorbed before adding more, and continuing to stir.

5 When the rice is about three-quarters cooked, stir in the bean purée (paste). Continue to cook the risotto, adding any stock that remains, until it has reached a creamy consistency and the rice is tender but still has a bit of "bite".

6 Add the reserved beans, with the mascarpone, Parmesan and rosemary, then season to taste with salt and pepper. Stir thoroughly, then cover and leave to stand for about 5 minutes so that the risotto absorbs the flavours fully and the rice finishes cooking. Serve with extra Parmesan, if you like.

VARIATION
Fresh thyme or marjoram could be used for this risotto instead of rosemary, if preferred. One of the great virtues of risotto is that it lends itself well to a range of equally tasty variations. Experiment with different herbs to make your own speciality dish.

FRESH HERB RISOTTO

HERE IS A RISOTTO TO CELEBRATE THE ABUNDANCE OF SUMMER HERBS. AN AROMATIC BLEND OF OREGANO, CHIVES, PARSLEY AND BASIL COMBINES WITH ARBORIO RICE TO MAKE A CREAMY AND SATISFYING MEAL.

3 Pour in the dry white wine and bring to the boil. Reduce the heat and cook for 10 minutes, or until all the wine has been absorbed.

4 Add the hot vegetable stock, a little at a time, waiting for each quantity to be absorbed before adding more, and stirring continuously. After 20–25 minutes the rice should be tender and creamy. Season well.

5 Add the herbs and wild rice; heat for 2 minutes, stirring frequently. Stir in two-thirds of the Parmesan and cook until melted. Serve sprinkled with the remaining Parmesan.

SERVES FOUR

INGREDIENTS
 90g/3½oz/½ cup wild rice
 15ml/1 tbsp butter
 15ml/1 tbsp olive oil
 1 small onion, finely chopped
 450g/1lb/2¼ cups arborio rice
 300ml/½ pint/1¼ cups dry
  white wine
 1.2 litres/2 pints/5 cups simmering
  vegetable stock
 45ml/3 tbsp chopped fresh oregano
 45ml/3 tbsp chopped fresh chives
 60ml/4 tbsp chopped fresh flat
  leaf parsley
 60ml/4 tbsp chopped fresh basil
 75g/3oz/1 cup freshly grated
  (shredded) Parmesan cheese
 salt and ground black pepper

1 Cook the wild rice in boiling salted water according to the instructions on the packet.

2 Heat the butter and oil in a large, heavy pan. When the butter has melted, add the onion and cook for 3 minutes. Add the arborio rice and cook for 2 minutes, stirring to coat.

COOK'S TIPS
• Risotto rice is essential to achieve the correct creamy texture in this dish. Other types of rice simply will not do.
• Fresh herbs are also a must, but you can use tarragon, chervil, marjoram or thyme instead of the ones listed here, if you prefer.

LEMON AND HERB RISOTTO CAKE

CHIVES AND PARSLEY COMBINE WITH THE RIND OF LEMON TO FLAVOUR THIS UNUSUAL MOZZARELLA AND RICE DISH. IT CAN BE SERVED AS A MAIN COURSE WITH SALAD, OR AS A SATISFYING SIDE DISH. IT'S ALSO GOOD SERVED COLD, AND PACKS WELL FOR PICNICS.

SERVES FOUR

INGREDIENTS
  oil, for greasing
  1 small leek, thinly sliced
  600ml/1 pint/2½ cups chicken stock
  225g/8oz/generous 1 cup risotto rice
  finely grated (shredded) rind of
    1 lemon
  30ml/2 tbsp chopped fresh chives
  30ml/2 tbsp chopped fresh parsley
  75g/3oz/¾ cup grated (shredded)
    mozzarella cheese
  salt and ground black pepper
  parsley and lemon wedges, to garnish

1 Preheat the oven to 200°C/400°F/ Gas 6. Use a pastry brush to lightly oil the base and sides of a 21cm/8½in round, loose-bottomed cake tin (pan).

2 Cook the leek in a large pan with 45ml/3 tbsp stock, stirring over a moderate heat, to soften. Add the rice and the remaining stock.

3 Bring to the boil. Cover the pan and simmer gently, stirring occasionally, for about 20 minutes, or until all the liquid is absorbed.

4 Stir in the lemon rind, herbs, cheese and seasoning. Spoon into the tin, cover with foil and bake for 30–35 minutes, or until lightly browned. Turn out and serve in slices, garnished with parsley and lemon wedges.

COOK'S TIP
The best type of rice to choose for this recipe is the Italian round-grain arborio rice, but if it is not available, use pudding rice instead.

THAI VEGETABLE AND CORIANDER CURRY WITH LEMON GRASS JASMINE RICE

AN ARRAY OF THAI SEASONINGS GIVES THIS RICH CURRY ITS MARVELLOUS FLAVOUR. LEMON GRASS ADDS ITS DELICATE SCENT TO THE CURRY AND THE JASMINE RICE ACCOMPANIMENT.

SERVES FOUR

INGREDIENTS
  10ml/2 tsp vegetable oil
  400ml/14fl oz/1⅔ cups coconut milk
  300ml/½ pint/1¼ cups good-quality
    vegetable stock
  225g/8oz new potatoes, halved or
    quartered, if large
  130g/4½oz baby corn cobs
  5ml/1 tsp golden caster (superfine)
    sugar
  185g/6½oz broccoli florets
  1 red (bell) pepper, seeded and
    sliced lengthways
  115g/4oz spinach, tough stalks
    removed and finely sliced
  30ml/2 tbsp chopped fresh
    coriander (cilantro)
  salt and ground black pepper
For the spice paste
  1 red chilli, seeded and chopped
  3 green chillies, seeded and chopped
  1 lemon grass stalk, outer leaves
    removed and lower 5cm/2in
    finely chopped
  2 shallots, chopped
  finely grated (shredded) rind of
    1 lime
  2 garlic cloves, chopped
  5ml/1 tsp ground coriander
  2.5ml/½ tsp ground cumin
  1cm/½in fresh galangal, finely
    chopped or 2.5ml/½ tsp dried
    (optional)
  45ml/3 tbsp chopped fresh coriander
    (cilantro)
For the rice
  225g/8oz/generous 1 cup jasmine
    rice, rinsed
  1 lemon grass stalk, outer leaves
    removed and cut into three pieces
  6 cardamom pods, bruised

1 Begin by making the spice paste. Place all the ingredients together in a food processor or blender and blend to a coarse paste.

2 Heat the oil in a large, heavy pan and fry the spice paste for 1–2 minutes, stirring constantly. Add the coconut milk and stock, and bring to the boil.

3 Reduce the heat, add the potatoes, and simmer for 15 minutes. Add the baby corn and seasoning, then cook for 2 minutes. Stir in the sugar, broccoli and red pepper, and cook for 2 minutes more, or until the vegetables are tender. Stir in the finely sliced spinach and 15ml/1 tbsp of the chopped fresh coriander. Cook for another 2 minutes.

4 Meanwhile, prepare the rice. Tip the rinsed rice into a large pan and add the pieces of lemon grass stalk and the cardamom pods. Pour over 475ml/ 16fl oz/2 cups water.

5 Bring to the boil, then reduce the heat, cover the pan and allow to cook for 10–15 minutes, or until the water is absorbed and the rice is tender and slightly sticky. Season with salt, leave to stand for 10 minutes, then fluff up the rice with a fork.

6 Remove the spices and serve the rice with the curry, sprinkled with the remaining fresh coriander.

COOK'S TIP
Galangal is the pungent, aromatic root of an Oriental plant. It can usually be found, in either fresh or dried form, in good Oriental supermarkets.

VARIATION
Try substituting other vegetables for the ones used here. Mushrooms and carrots would both work well.

PANSOTTI WITH HERBS AND CHEESE

HERB-FLAVOURED PASTA ENCLOSES A FILLING OF RICOTTA CHEESE, BASIL, PARSLEY, MARJORAM AND GARLIC. THE PANSOTTI ARE THEN SERVED WITH A RICH AND SATISFYING WALNUT SAUCE – HEAVENLY.

SERVES SIX TO EIGHT

INGREDIENTS

For the herb-flavoured pasta
  300g/11oz/2¾ cups flour
  3 eggs
  5ml/1 tsp salt
  3 small handfuls of fresh herbs,
    finely chopped
  flour, for dusting
  50g/2oz/¼ cup butter
  freshly grated (shredded) Parmesan
    cheese, to serve

For the filling
  250g/9oz/generous 1 cup ricotta cheese
  150g/5oz/1⅔ cups freshly grated
    (shredded) Parmesan cheese
  1 large handful fresh basil leaves,
    finely chopped
  1 large handful fresh flat leaf parsley,
    finely chopped
  a few sprigs fresh marjoram or
    oregano, leaves removed and
    finely chopped
  1 garlic clove, crushed
  1 small egg
  salt and ground black pepper

For the sauce
  90g/3½oz/½ cup shelled walnuts
  1 garlic clove
  60ml/4 tbsp extra virgin olive oil
  120ml/4fl oz/½ cup double
    (heavy) cream

1 Mound the flour on the work surface and make a deep well in the centre.

2 Crack the eggs into the well, then add the salt and herbs. With a table knife, mix the eggs, salt and herbs together, then start incorporating the flour from the sides of the well.

3 As soon as the mixture is no longer liquid dip your fingers in the flour and use them to work the ingredients into a sticky dough. Press the dough into a ball and knead it as you would bread, for 10 minutes until smooth and elastic. Wrap in clear film and leave to rest at room temperature for 20 minutes.

4 To make the filling, put the ricotta, Parmesan, herbs, garlic and egg in a bowl with salt and pepper to taste and beat well to mix.

5 To make the sauce, put the walnuts, garlic clove and olive oil in a food processor and process to a paste, adding up to 120ml/4fl oz/½ cup warm water through the feeder tube to lighten the consistency.

6 Spoon the mixture into a large bowl and add the cream. Beat well to mix, then add salt and pepper to taste.

7 Using a pasta machine, roll out one-quarter of the pasta into a 90cm/36in strip. Cut the strip with a sharp knife into two 45cm/18in lengths (you can do this during rolling if the strip gets too long to manage).

8 Using a 5cm/2in square ravioli cutter, cut eight or nine squares from one of the pasta strips. Using a teaspoon, put a mound of filling in the centre of each square.

9 Brush a little water around the edge of each square, then fold the square diagonally in half over the filling to make a triangular shape. Press the edges gently to seal.

10 Spread out the pansotti on clean, floured dish towels, sprinkle lightly with flour and leave to dry. Repeat the process with the remaining dough to make 64–80 pansotti altogether.

11 Cook the pansotti in a large pan of salted boiling water for 4–5 minutes. Meanwhile, put the walnut sauce in a large, warmed bowl and add a ladleful of the pasta cooking water to thin it down. Melt the butter in a small pan until sizzling.

12 Drain the pansotti and tip them into the bowl of walnut sauce. Drizzle the butter over them, toss well, then sprinkle with Parmesan. Alternatively, toss the pansotti in the melted butter, spoon into warmed individual bowls and drizzle over the sauce. Serve immediately, with more Parmesan offered separately.

TAGLIATELLE <u>WITH</u> HERBS

IN SUMMER, WHEN HERBS ARE PLENTIFUL, ENJOY THIS SIMPLE PASTA DISH THAT IS SO FULL OF FLAVOUR. ROSEMARY, PARSLEY, MINT, SAGE, BASIL, BAY AND GARLIC ARE ALL HERE, MERGING TOGETHER TO CREATE A LIGHT, AND TASTY MEAL.

SERVES SIX

INGREDIENTS

3 rosemary sprigs
1 small handful fresh flat leaf parsley
5–6 fresh mint leaves
5–6 fresh sage leaves
8–10 large fresh basil leaves
30ml/2 tbsp extra virgin olive oil
50g/2oz/¼ cup butter
1 shallot, finely chopped
2 garlic cloves, finely chopped
pinch of chilli powder, to taste
400g/14oz fresh egg tagliatelle
1 bay leaf
120ml/4fl oz/½ cup dry white wine
90–120ml/6–8 tbsp vegetable stock
salt and ground black pepper
basil leaves, to garnish

1 Strip the rosemary and parsley leaves from their stalks and chop them together with the other fresh herbs.

2 Heat the oil and half the butter in a large pan. Add the shallot, garlic and chilli powder. Cook on a very low heat, stirring frequently, for 2–3 minutes.

3 Cook the fresh pasta in a large pan of boiling salted water according to the packet instructions.

4 Add the chopped herbs and the bay leaf to the shallot mixture and stir for 2–3 minutes, then add the wine and increase the heat. Boil rapidly for 1–2 minutes, or until reduced. Lower the heat, add the stock and simmer gently for 1–2 minutes. Season.

5 Drain the pasta and add it to the herb mixture. Toss well to mix and remove and discard the bay leaf.

6 Put the remaining butter in a warmed large bowl, tip the dressed pasta into it and toss well to mix. Serve immediately, garnished with basil.

VERMICELLI WITH HERB FRITTATA

HERE, ROASTED RED PEPPER, BASIL, PARSLEY, GARLIC AND ONION CREATE A FULL AND FRESH FLAVOUR. IT MAKES A SUBSTANTIAL AND TASTY LUNCHEON DISH AND IS ALSO EXCELLENT FOR PICNICS.

SERVES FOUR TO SIX

INGREDIENTS

    50g/2oz dried vermicelli
    6 eggs
    60ml/4 tbsp double (heavy) cream
    1 handful fresh basil
      leaves, chopped
    1 handful fresh flat leaf
      parsley, chopped
    75g/3oz/1 cup freshly grated
      (shredded) Parmesan cheese
    25g/1oz/2 tbsp butter
    15ml/1 tbsp olive oil
    1 onion, finely sliced
    3 large pieces bottled roasted red
      (bell) pepper, drained, rinsed,
      dried and cut into strips
    1 garlic clove, crushed
    salt and ground black pepper
    rocket (arugula) leaves, to serve

1 Preheat the oven to 190°C/375°F/ Gas 5. Cook the pasta in a pan of boiling salted water for 8 minutes.

2 Meanwhile, break the eggs into a bowl and add the cream and herbs. Whisk in about two-thirds of the grated Parmesan and add salt and pepper to taste.

3 Drain the pasta well and allow to cool; snip it into short lengths with scissors. Add to the egg mixture and whisk again.

4 Melt the butter in the oil in a large, ovenproof, non-stick frying pan. Add the onion and cook gently, stirring frequently, until softened. Add the pepper and garlic.

5 Pour the egg and pasta mixture into the pan and stir well. Cook over a low to medium heat, without stirring, for 3–5 minutes, or until the frittata is just set underneath.

6 Sprinkle over the remaining Parmesan and bake in the oven for 5 minutes or until set.

7 Before serving, leave to stand for at least 5 minutes. Cut into wedges and serve warm or cold, accompanied by rocket leaves.

SUMMER HERB RICOTTA FLAN

SIMPLE TO MAKE AND INFUSED WITH AROMATIC BASIL, CHIVES AND OREGANO, THIS DELICATE FLAN MAKES A DELIGHTFUL LUNCH DISH, ACCOMPANIED BY AN OLIVE AND GARLIC TAPENADE.

SERVES FOUR

INGREDIENTS
    olive oil, for greasing and glazing
    800g/1¾lb/3½ cups ricotta cheese
    75g/3oz/1 cup finely grated
        (shredded) Parmesan cheese
    3 eggs, separated
    60ml/4 tbsp torn fresh basil leaves
    60ml/4 tbsp chopped fresh chives
    45ml/3 tbsp fresh oregano leaves
    2.5ml/½ tsp salt
    ground black pepper
    2.5ml/½ tsp paprika
    fresh herb leaves, to garnish
For the tapenade
    400g/14oz/3½ cups pitted black
        olives, rinsed and halved,
        reserving a few whole olives to
        garnish (optional)
    5 garlic cloves, crushed
    75ml/2½fl oz/⅓ cup olive oil

1 Preheat the oven to 180°C/350°F/ Gas 4 and then lightly grease a 23cm/ 9in springform cake tin (pan) with olive oil. Mix together the ricotta, Parmesan and egg yolks in a food processor. Add all the herbs, and the salt and pepper, and blend until smooth and creamy.

2 Whisk the egg whites in a large bowl until they form soft peaks. Gently fold the egg whites into the ricotta mixture, taking care not to knock out too much air. Spoon the ricotta mixture into the tin and smooth the top.

3 Bake for 1 hour 20 minutes, or until the flan has risen and the top is golden. Remove from the oven and brush lightly with olive oil, then sprinkle with paprika. Cool before removing from the tin.

4 Make the tapenade. Place the olives and garlic in a food processor or blender and process until finely chopped. Gradually add the olive oil and blend to a coarse paste, then transfer to a serving bowl. Garnish the flan with fresh herb leaves and serve with the tapenade.

RED ONION AND GOAT'S CHEESE PASTRIES

FRESH THYME ADDS A TASTY EDGE TO THE RED ONION IN THESE SCRUMPTIOUS PASTRIES. RING THE CHANGES BY SPREADING THE PASTRY BASE WITH PESTO OR TAPENADE BEFORE YOU ADD THE FILLING.

SERVES FOUR

INGREDIENTS
    15ml/1 tbsp olive oil
    450g/1lb red onions, sliced
    30ml/2 tbsp fresh thyme or 10ml/
        2 tsp dried
    15ml/1 tbsp balsamic vinegar
    425g/15oz packet ready-rolled puff
        pastry, thawed if frozen
    115g/4oz goat's cheese, cubed
    1 egg, beaten
    salt and ground black pepper
    fresh oregano sprigs, to garnish
        (optional)
    mixed green salad leaves, to serve

1 Heat the oil in a large, heavy frying pan, add the onions and fry over a gentle heat for 10 minutes, or until softened, stirring occasionally. Add the thyme, seasoning and vinegar, and cook for another 5 minutes. Remove the pan from the heat and leave to cool.

2 Preheat the oven to 220°C/425°F/ Gas 7. Unroll the puff pastry and, using a 15cm/6in plate as a guide, cut four rounds. Place the pastry rounds on a dampened baking sheet and, using the point of a knife, score a border, 2cm/¾in inside the edge of each round. (Do not cut through the pastry.)

3 Divide the onions among the pastry rounds and top with the goat's cheese. Brush the edge of each round with beaten egg.

4 Bake the pastries for 25–30 minutes, or until they are golden. Garnish with oregano sprigs, if you like, before serving with mixed salad leaves.

FRIED PEPPERS WITH CHEESE AND PARSLEY

FETA CHEESE GOES PARTICULARLY WELL WITH PARSLEY AND A HINT OF CHILLI, AND IS USED HERE AS A FILLING FOR RIPE PEPPERS IN A TRADITIONAL BULGARIAN DISH. RED, GREEN OR YELLOW PEPPERS ARE EQUALLY DELICIOUS SERVED THIS WAY.

SERVES TWO TO FOUR

INGREDIENTS
    4 long (bell) peppers
    50g/2oz/½ cup plain (all-purpose)
      flour, seasoned
    1 egg, beaten
    olive oil, for shallow frying
    cucumber and tomato salad, to serve
For the filling
    1 egg
    90g/3½oz feta cheese, finely
      crumbled
    30ml/2 tbsp chopped fresh parsley
    1 small fresh chilli, seeded and
      finely chopped

1 Slit open the peppers lengthways, scoop out the seeds. Remove the cores, leaving the peppers in one piece.

2 Carefully open out the peppers and place under a preheated grill (broiler), skin-side uppermost. Cook until the skin is charred and blackened. Place the peppers on a plate, cover with clear film and leave for 10 minutes.

3 Using a sharp knife, carefully peel away the skin from the peppers.

4 In a bowl, thoroughly mix all the filling ingredients together. Divide evenly among the four peppers.

5 Reshape the peppers to look whole. Dip them into the seasoned flour, then the egg, then the flour again.

6 Fry the peppers gently in a little olive oil for 6–8 minutes, turning once, or until golden brown and the filling is set. Drain the peppers on kitchen paper before serving with a cucumber and tomato salad.

COOK'S TIP
Feta cheese is traditionally made from ewe's or goat's milk, although it is now sometimes made from cow's milk. It keeps well if stored in a screw-top jar or polythene wrapper in the fridge.

BAKED FENNEL <u>WITH A</u> CRUMB CRUST

GARLIC AND PARSLEY BLEND PERFECTLY WITH THE DELICATE, ANISEED FLAVOUR OF FENNEL IN THIS TASTY GRATIN. IT GOES WELL WITH PASTA DISHES AND RISOTTOS.

SERVES FOUR

INGREDIENTS

3 fennel bulbs, cut lengthways
  into quarters
30ml/2 tbsp olive oil
1 garlic clove, chopped
50g/2oz/1 cup day-old wholemeal
  (whole-wheat) breadcrumbs
30ml/2 tbsp chopped fresh flat
  leaf parsley
salt and ground black pepper
fennel leaves, to garnish (optional)

VARIATION

To make a cheese-topped version of this dish, simply add 60ml/4 tbsp finely grated strong-flavoured cheese, such as mature Cheddar, Red Leicester or Parmesan, to the breadcrumb mixture in step 4. Sprinkle the mixture over the fennel as described.

1 Cook the fennel in a pan of boiling salted water for 10 minutes, or until just tender.

2 Drain the fennel quarters and place them in a baking dish or roasting pan, then brush them all over with half of the olive oil.

3 Preheat the oven to 190°C/375°F/ Gas 5.

4 In a small bowl, mix together the garlic, breadcrumbs and parsley with the rest of the oil. Sprinkle the mixture evenly over the fennel, then season well with salt and pepper.

5 Bake for 30 minutes, or until the fennel is tender and the breadcrumbs are crisp and golden. Serve hot, garnished with a few fennel leaves, if you wish.

MINTED POTATO AND RED PEPPER FRITTATA

FRESH MINT TASTES WONDERFUL WITH NEW POTATOES. IN THIS ITALIAN-STYLE OMELETTE IT COMBINES WITH GARLIC, ONION AND BRIGHT RED PEPPERS TO MAKE A LIGHT AND TEMPTING LUNCH DISH THAT IS SIMPLY BURSTING WITH FLAVOUR.

SERVES THREE TO FOUR

INGREDIENTS

    450g/1lb small new or salad potatoes
    6 eggs
    30ml/2 tbsp chopped fresh mint
    30ml/2 tbsp olive oil
    1 onion, chopped
    2 garlic cloves, crushed
    2 red (bell) peppers, seeded and
      roughly chopped
    salt and ground black pepper
    mint sprigs, to garnish

1 Cook the potatoes in their skins in boiling salted water until just tender. Drain, cool slightly, then slice thickly.

2 Whisk together the eggs, chopped fresh mint and seasoning in a bowl, then set aside. Heat the olive oil in a large frying pan that can be used under the grill (broiler).

3 Add the onion, garlic, peppers and potatoes to the pan and cook, stirring occasionally, for 5 minutes.

4 Pour the egg mixture over the vegetables in the frying pan and stir gently with a wooden spoon to ensure the egg is evenly distributed.

5 Push the mixture towards the centre of the pan as it cooks to allow the liquid egg to run on to the base. Meanwhile preheat the grill.

6 When the frittata is lightly set, place the frying pan under the hot grill for 2–3 minutes until the top is a light golden brown colour.

7 Serve the frittata hot or cold, cut into wedges. Garnish with extra sprigs of mint.

FRITTATA WITH TOMATOES AND THYME

A FRITTATA IS AN ITALIAN OMELETTE THAT IS COOKED UNTIL FIRM ENOUGH TO BE CUT INTO WEDGES. SUN-DRIED TOMATOES AND A HINT OF THYME GIVE THIS FRITTATA A DISTINCTIVE FLAVOUR.

SERVES THREE TO FOUR

INGREDIENTS

    6 sun-dried tomatoes
    60ml/4 tbsp olive oil
    1 small onion, finely chopped
    60ml/4 tbsp fresh thyme leaves
    6 eggs
    50g/2oz/⅔ cup freshly grated
      (shredded) Parmesan cheese
    salt and ground black pepper
    sprigs of thyme, to garnish
    shavings of Parmesan, to serve

1 Place the tomatoes in a small bowl and pour on enough hot water just to cover them. Leave to soak for about 15 minutes. Lift the tomatoes out of the water and pat dry on kitchen paper. Reserve the soaking water. Cut the tomatoes into thin strips.

2 Heat the oil in a large, non-stick frying pan. Stir in the chopped onion and cook for 5–6 minutes, or until softened and golden.

3 Stir in the sun-dried tomatoes and thyme, and cook over a moderate heat for a further 2–3 minutes, stirring from time to time. Season with salt and ground black pepper.

4 Break the eggs into a bowl and beat lightly. Stir in 45ml/3 tbsp of the tomato soaking water and the Parmesan. Raise the heat under the pan. When the oil is sizzling, add the eggs. Mix quickly into the other ingredients, then stop stirring. Lower the heat to moderate and cook for 4–5 minutes, or until the base is golden and the top puffed.

5 Take a large plate, place it upside down over the pan and, holding it firmly with oven gloves, turn the pan and the frittata over on to it. Slide the frittata back into the pan, and continue cooking for 3–4 minutes, or until golden on the second side. Remove from the heat. Cut into wedges, garnish with thyme and serve with Parmesan.

COOK'S TIP
If you find it difficult to slide the frittata on to a plate, simply place the pan under a hot grill to brown the top, protecting the handle if necessary.

BAKED HERB CRÊPES

ADD FRESH HERBS TO MAKE CRÊPES SOMETHING SPECIAL, THEN FILL WITH SPINACH, PINE NUTS AND RICOTTA CHEESE FLAVOURED WITH BASIL. DELICIOUS SERVED WITH A GARLICKY TOMATO SAUCE.

SERVES FOUR

INGREDIENTS
  25g/1oz/½ cup chopped fresh herbs
  15ml/1 tbsp sunflower oil, plus extra
    for frying
  120ml/4fl oz/½ cup milk
  3 eggs
  25g/1oz/¼ cup plain (all-purpose)
    flour
  pinch of salt
  oil, for greasing
For the sauce
  30ml/2 tbsp olive oil
  1 small onion, chopped
  2 garlic cloves, crushed
  400g/14oz can chopped tomatoes
  pinch of soft light brown sugar
For the filling
  450g/1lb fresh spinach, cooked
    and drained
  175g/6oz/¾ cup ricotta cheese
  25g/1oz/¼ cup pine nuts, toasted
  5 sun-dried tomato halves in olive
    oil, drained and chopped
  30ml/2 tbsp chopped fresh basil
  salt, nutmeg and ground
    black pepper
  4 egg whites

3 To make the sauce, heat the oil in a small pan, add the onion and garlic and cook gently for 5 minutes. Add the tomatoes and sugar and cook for about 10 minutes, or until thickened. Purée in a blender, then sieve and set aside.

4 To make the filling, mix together the spinach with the ricotta, pine nuts, tomatoes and basil. Season with salt, nutmeg and pepper.

5 Preheat the oven to 190°C/375°F/ Gas 5. Whisk the egg whites until stiff. Fold one-third into the spinach mixture, then gently fold in the rest.

6 Place one crêpe at a time on a lightly oiled baking sheet, add a spoonful of filling and fold into quarters. Bake for 12 minutes until set. Reheat the sauce and serve with the crêpes.

1 To make the crêpes, place the herbs and oil in a food processor and blend until smooth. Add the milk, eggs, flour and salt and process again until smooth. Leave to rest for 30 minutes.

2 Heat a small, non-stick frying pan and add a small amount of oil. Add a ladleful of batter. Swirl around to cover the base. Cook for 2 minutes, turn and cook for 2 minutes. Make seven more crêpes.

BRESAOLA AND ROCKET PIZZA

HERE IS A QUICK AND TASTY PIZZA SPREAD WITH PESTO — A MIXTURE OF GROUND BASIL, PARSLEY AND PINE NUTS — AND TOPPED WITH GARLIC, TOMATOES, WILD MUSHROOMS AND BRESAOLA. CRISP, PEPPERY ROCKET GIVES IT A FRESH FINISH.

SERVES FOUR

INGREDIENTS

150g/5oz packet pizza base mix
120ml/4fl oz/½ cup lukewarm water
flour, for dusting
225g/8oz/3¼ cups mixed
  wild mushrooms
25g/1oz/2 tbsp butter
2 garlic cloves, coarsely chopped
60ml/4 tbsp pesto
8 slices bresaola
4 tomatoes, sliced
75g/3oz/scant ⅓ cup full-fat
  cream cheese
25g/1oz rocket (arugula)
salt and ground black pepper

1 Preheat the oven to 200°C/400°F/ Gas 6. Tip the packet of pizza base mix into a large mixing bowl and pour in enough of the lukewarm water to mix to a soft, not sticky, dough.

2 Turn out the dough on to a lightly floured surface and knead for about 5 minutes, or until smooth and elastic. Divide the dough into two equal pieces, knead lightly to form two balls, then pat out the balls of dough into flat rounds.

COOK'S TIP
If you are in a hurry, buy two ready-made pizza bases instead of the pizza mix and bake for 10 minutes.

3 Roll out each piece of the pizza dough on a lightly floured surface to a 23cm/9in round and then transfer to baking sheets.

4 Slice the wild mushrooms. Melt the butter in a frying pan and cook the garlic for 2 minutes. Add the sliced mushrooms and cook them over a high heat for about 5 minutes, or until they have softened but are not overcooked. Season to taste with salt and ground black pepper.

5 Spread pesto on the pizza bases, leaving a 2cm/¾in border around the edge of each one. Arrange the bresaola and tomato slices around the rim of the pesto layer, then spoon the cooked garlic mushrooms into the centre.

6 Dot the cream cheese on top of the pizzas and then bake in the preheated oven for 15–18 minutes, or until the bases are crisp and the cheese has just melted. Top each pizza with a handful of the rocket leaves just before serving. Serve the pizzas at once.

ROCKET AND TOMATO PIZZA

GARLIC AND BASIL FLAVOUR A TOMATO SAUCE THAT BLENDS BEAUTIFULLY WITH CREAMY MOZZARELLA.
ROCKET, WITH ITS PRONOUNCED FLAVOUR, ADDS THE FINAL TOUCH.

2 Cover the dough with the upturned bowl or a dish towel and leave to rest for about 5 minutes, then knead for a further 5 minutes, or until smooth and elastic. Place in a lightly oiled bowl and cover with clear film. Leave in a warm place for about 45 minutes, or until doubled in size.

3 Preheat the oven to 220°C/425°F/ Gas 7. To make the topping, heat the oil in a frying pan and fry the garlic for 1 minute. Add the canned tomatoes and sugar, and cook for 5–7 minutes, or until reduced and thickened. Stir in the basil and seasoning, then set aside.

4 Knead the risen dough lightly, then roll out to form a rough 30cm/12in round. Place on a lightly oiled baking sheet and push up the edges of the dough to form a shallow, even rim.

SERVES TWO

INGREDIENTS
    10ml/2 tsp olive oil, plus extra
       for drizzling and greasing
    1 garlic clove, crushed
    150g/5oz canned chopped tomatoes
    2.5ml/½ tsp sugar
    30ml/2 tbsp torn fresh basil leaves
    2 tomatoes, seeded and chopped
    150g/5oz mozzarella cheese, sliced
    20g/¾oz rocket (arugula) leaves
    coarse salt and ground black pepper
For the pizza base
    225g/8oz/2 cups strong white bread
       flour, sifted, plus extra for dusting
    5ml/1 tsp salt
    2.5ml/½ tsp easy-blend (rapid-rise)
       dried yeast
    15ml/1 tbsp olive oil, plus extra
       for greasing

1 To make the pizza base, place the flour, salt and easy-blend dried yeast in a large bowl. Make a well in the centre and add the oil and 150ml/¼ pint/⅔ cup warm water. Mix with a round-bladed knife to form a soft dough. Turn out on to a lightly floured work surface and knead for 5 minutes.

5 Spoon the tomato mixture over the pizza base, then top with the chopped fresh tomatoes, and the mozzarella. Season, then drizzle with olive oil. Bake in the top of the oven for 10–12 minutes, or until crisp and golden. Scatter with rocket and serve.

TOMATO, FENNEL AND PARSLEY PIZZA

THIS PIZZA RELIES ON THE WINNING COMBINATION OF TOMATOES, FENNEL AND PARSLEY. THE FENNEL ADDS BOTH A CRISP TEXTURE AND A DISTINCTIVE FLAVOUR.

SERVES TWO TO THREE

INGREDIENTS

1 fennel bulb
45ml/3 tbsp garlic oil
1 pizza base, 25–30cm/10–12in
  diameter
30ml/2 tbsp chopped fresh flat leaf
  parsley
50g/2oz/½ cup grated (shredded)
  mozzarella cheese
50g/2oz/⅔ cup freshly grated
  (shredded) Parmesan cheese
salt and ground black pepper
For the tomato sauce
15ml/1 tbsp olive oil
1 onion, finely chopped
1 garlic clove, crushed
400g/14oz can chopped tomatoes
15ml/1 tbsp tomato purée (paste)
15ml/1 tbsp chopped fresh mixed
  herbs, such as parsley, thyme, basil
  and oregano
pinch of sugar
salt and ground black pepper

1 To make the tomato sauce, heat the oil in a pan and fry the onion and garlic until softened. Add the tomatoes, tomato purée (paste), herbs, sugar and seasoning. Simmer, stirring occasionally, until the tomatoes have reduced to a thick pulp.

2 Preheat the oven to 220°C/425°F/ Gas 7. Trim and quarter the fennel bulb lengthways. Remove the core and slice thinly.

3 Heat 30ml/2 tbsp of the oil in a frying pan and sauté the fennel for 4–5 minutes, or until just tender. Season.

4 Brush the pizza base with the remaining oil and spread over the tomato sauce. Spoon the fennel on top and scatter over the flat leaf parsley.

5 Mix together the mozzarella and Parmesan and sprinkle evenly over the top of the pizza. Bake for 15–20 minutes, or until crisp and golden. Serve immediately.

breads & bakes

Fresh herbs can bring diversity to all your breads and baking.

Mediterranean breads rely heavily on pungent herbs like rosemary, basil

and oregano, whether they're kneaded into the dough or simply

sprinkled over before baking, working their magic on both appearance

and flavour. For loaves or little buns, try adding herbs like sage, parsley

and chives, great for snacking with cheese or taking on picnics. For

sweet bakes and biscuits, you can't beat the subtle sweetness of herbs,

such as lavender, heightened with the fresh tang of lemon.

ITALIAN FLAT BREAD WITH ROSEMARY

ROSEMARY LEAVES ADD THEIR UNMISTAKABLE FLAVOUR TO THE TUSCAN VERSION OF AN ITALIAN FLAT BREAD. IT CAN BE ROLLED TO VARYING THICKNESSES TO GIVE EITHER A CRISP OR SOFT FINISH.

MAKES ONE LARGE LOAF

INGREDIENTS
   60ml/4 tbsp extra virgin olive oil,
     plus extra for greasing
   350g/12oz/3 cups unbleached white
     bread flour, plus extra for dusting
   2.5ml/½ tsp salt
   15g/½oz fresh yeast
   200ml/7fl oz/scant 1 cup
     lukewarm water
For the topping
   30ml/2 tbsp extra virgin olive oil
   30ml/2 tbsp fresh rosemary leaves
   coarse salt, for sprinkling

1 Lightly oil a baking sheet. Sift the flour and salt into a bowl and make a well in the centre. Cream the yeast with half the water. Add to the well with the remaining water and oil and mix to a soft dough. Turn out on to a lightly floured surface and knead for 10 minutes, until smooth and elastic.

2 Place the dough in a lightly oiled bowl, cover with a layer of lightly oiled clear film and leave to rise in a warm place for about 1 hour, or until it has doubled in bulk.

3 Knock back (punch down) the dough, turn out on to a lightly floured surface and knead gently. Roll to a 30 × 20cm/12 × 8in rectangle and place on the prepared baking sheet. Brush with some of the olive oil for the topping and cover with lightly oiled clear film.

4 Leave the dough to rise once again in a warm place for about 20 minutes. Brush with the remaining olive oil, prick all over with a fork and sprinkle with fresh rosemary leaves and coarse salt. Leave to rise again in a warm place for a further 15 minutes.

5 Meanwhile, preheat the oven to 200°C/400°F/Gas 6. Bake the loaf for 30 minutes, or until light golden. Transfer to a wire rack to cool slightly. Serve while still warm.

SAFFRON FOCACCIA <u>WITH</u> ROSEMARY TOPPING

A DAZZLING YELLOW BREAD WITH A DISTINCTIVE FLAVOUR, THIS SAFFRON FOCACCIA IS TOPPED WITH GARLIC, ONION, ROSEMARY AND OLIVES. IT MAKES A TASTY SNACK OR ACCOMPANIMENT.

MAKES ONE LOAF

INGREDIENTS
 pinch of saffron threads
 150ml/¼ pint/⅔ cup boiling water
 225g/8oz/2 cups plain (all-purpose)
  flour, plus extra for dusting
 2.5ml/½ tsp salt
 5ml/1 tsp easy-blend (rapid-rise)
  dried yeast
 15ml/1 tbsp olive oil, plus extra
  for greasing
For the topping
 2 garlic cloves, sliced
 1 red onion, cut into thin wedges
 fresh rosemary sprigs
 12 black olives, pitted and
  coarsely chopped
 15ml/1 tbsp olive oil

1 In a jug, infuse (steep) the saffron in the boiling water. Leave until lukewarm.

2 Place the flour, salt, yeast and oil in a food processor. Turn on, gradually add the saffron liquid until the dough forms a ball. Alternatively, put the dry ingredients into a bowl, make a well in the centre and pour in the liquids. Gradually mix in.

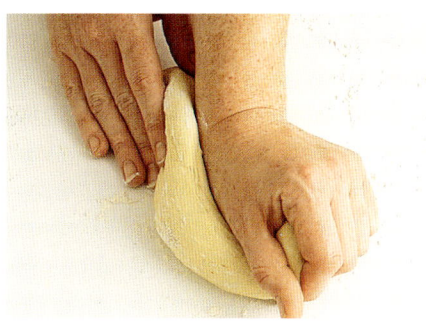

3 Transfer the dough on to a lightly floured work surface and knead for 10–15 minutes, or until smooth and elastic. Place in a bowl, cover and leave in a warm place for 30–40 minutes, or until the dough has doubled in bulk. Lightly grease a baking sheet and set aside.

4 Knock back (punch down) the risen dough on a lightly floured surface and roll out into an oval shape about 1cm/½in thick. Place on the prepared baking sheet and then leave to rise in a warm place for 20–30 minutes.

5 Preheat the oven to 200°C/400°F/ Gas 6. Use your fingers to press small indentations in the dough.

6 Cover the dough with the garlic, onion, rosemary and olives, brush lightly with the olive oil, and bake the loaf in the oven for about 25 minutes, or until it sounds hollow when tapped underneath.

7 Transfer the cooked loaf to a wire rack to cool. Serve the focaccia in slices or wedges.

POPPY-SEEDED BLOOMER

THIS SATISFYING WHITE BREAD HAS A CRUNCHY, POPPY-SEED TOPPING. IT IS MADE BY A SLOWER RISING METHOD AND WITH LESS YEAST THAN USUAL. THIS PRODUCES A LONGER-KEEPING LOAF WITH A FULLER FLAVOUR. THE DOUGH TAKES ABOUT 8 HOURS TO RISE.

MAKES ONE LOAF

INGREDIENTS
  oil, for greasing
  675g/1½lb/6 cups unbleached strong
    white bread flour, plus extra for dusting
  10ml/2 tsp salt
  15g/½oz fresh yeast
  430ml/15fl oz/1⅞ cups water
For the topping
  2.5ml/½ tsp salt
  30ml/2 tbsp water
  poppy seeds, for sprinkling

1 Lightly grease a baking sheet. Sift the flour and salt together into a large bowl and make a well in the centre.

2 Mix the yeast and 150ml/¼ pint/ ⅔ cup of the water in a bowl. Mix in the remaining water and add to the centre of the flour. Mix it in, gradually incorporating the surrounding flour, until the mixture forms a firm dough.

3 Turn out on to a lightly floured surface and knead the dough very well, for at least 10 minutes, or until smooth and elastic.

4 Place the dough in a lightly oiled bowl, cover with lightly oiled clear film and leave to rise, at cool room temperature, about 15–18°C/60–65°F, for 5–6 hours, or until doubled in bulk.

5 Knock back (punch down) the dough, turn out on to a lightly floured surface and knead it thoroughly and quite hard for about 5 minutes. Return the dough to the bowl, and re-cover. Leave to rise, at cool room temperature, for a further 2 hours or slightly longer.

6 Knock back again and repeat the thorough kneading. Leave the dough to rest for 5 minutes, then roll out on a lightly floured surface into a rectangle 2.5cm/1in thick. Roll the dough up from one long side and shape it into a square-ended thick baton shape, about 33 × 13cm/13 × 5in.

7 Place it seam-side up on a baking sheet, cover and leave to rest for 15 minutes. Turn over. Plump up by tucking the dough under the sides and ends. Using a sharp knife, cut six diagonal slashes on the top.

8 Leave to rest, covered, in a warm place, for 10 minutes. Meanwhile, preheat the oven to 230°C/450°F/Gas 8.

9 Mix the salt and water together and brush this glaze over the bread. Sprinkle with poppy seeds.

10 Spray the oven with water. Bake the bread immediately for 20 minutes, then reduce the oven temperature to 200°C/ 400°F/Gas 6; bake for 25 minutes more, or until golden. Transfer to a wire rack to cool.

VARIATION
For a more rustic loaf, replace up to half the flour with wholemeal (whole-wheat) bread flour.

COOK'S TIPS
• The traditional cracked, crusty appearance of this loaf is difficult to achieve in a domestic oven. However, you can get a similar result by spraying the oven with water before baking.
• If the underneath of the loaf is not very crusty at the end of baking, turn the loaf over on the baking sheet, switch off the heat and leave in the oven for a further 5–10 minutes.

WARM HERBY BREAD

THIS MOUTH-WATERING, ITALIAN-STYLE BREAD, FLAVOURED WITH BASIL, ROSEMARY, OLIVE OIL AND SUN-DRIED TOMATOES, IS ABSOLUTELY DELICIOUS SERVED WARM WITH FRESH SALADS AND SLICED SALAMI OR PROSCIUTTO. THE OLIVE OIL NOT ONLY LENDS A DELICIOUS FLAVOUR TO THE BREAD, BUT ALSO HELPS IT TO KEEP FRESH FOR LONGER.

3 As the mixture becomes stiffer, bring it together with your hands. Mix to a soft but not sticky dough, adding a little extra water if needed.

4 Turn the dough out on to a lightly floured surface and knead for 5 minutes until smooth and elastic. Put back into the bowl, cover loosely with oiled clear film and then put in a warm place for 30–40 minutes, or until doubled in size.

5 Knead again until smooth and elastic, then cut into three pieces. Shape each into an oval loaf about 18cm/7in long, and arrange on oiled baking sheets. Slash the top of each loaf with a knife in a criss-cross pattern.

MAKES THREE LOAVES

INGREDIENTS
    20g/¾oz fresh yeast or 15ml/1 tbsp
    dried yeast
    5ml/1 tsp caster (superfine) sugar
    900ml/1½ pints/3¾ cups warm water
    1.3kg/3lb/12 cups strong white bread
    flour, plus extra for dusting
    15ml/1 tbsp salt
    75ml/5 tbsp mixed fresh chopped
    basil and rosemary leaves
    50g/2oz/1 cup drained sun-dried
    tomatoes, roughly chopped
    150ml/¼ pint/⅔ cup extra virgin olive
    oil, plus extra for greasing and brushing
To finish
    15ml/1 tbsp rosemary leaves
    sea salt flakes

1 Cream the fresh yeast with the sugar, and gradually stir in 150ml/¼ pint/ ⅔ cup warm water. If you are using dried yeast, put the sugar into a small bowl, pour on the same amount of warm water, then sprinkle the yeast over the top. Leave the mixture in a warm place for 10–15 minutes, or until it has reached a frothy consistency.

2 Put the flour, salt, chopped basil and rosemary leaves, and chopped sun-dried tomatoes into a large mixing bowl. Add the olive oil together with the frothy yeast mixture, then gradually mix in the remaining warm water with a spoon.

6 Loosely cover and leave in a warm place for 15–20 minutes, or until well risen. Preheat the oven to 220°C/425°F/ Gas 7. Brush the loaves with a little olive oil and sprinkle with rosemary leaves and salt flakes. Cook for about 25 minutes, or until golden brown. The bases should sound hollow when they are tapped.

SAFFRON AND BASIL BREADSTICKS

THESE TASTY BREADSTICKS HAVE THE DELICATE AROMA AND FLAVOUR OF SAFFRON, AS WELL AS ITS RICH YELLOW COLOUR. THEY ARE IDEAL AS AN ACCOMPANIMENT TO SOUPS OR SALADS OR AS A SNACK.

MAKES THIRTY-TWO

INGREDIENTS
- generous pinch of saffron strands
- 30ml/2 tbsp hot water
- 450g/1lb/4 cups strong white bread flour, plus extra for dusting
- 5ml/1 tsp salt
- 10ml/2 tsp easy-blend (rapid-rise) dried yeast
- 300ml/½ pint/1¼ cups lukewarm water
- 45ml/3 tbsp olive oil, plus extra for greasing
- 45ml/3 tbsp chopped fresh basil

1 In a small bowl, infuse (steep) the saffron strands in the hot water for 10 minutes.

2 Sift the flour and salt into a large mixing bowl. Stir in the yeast, then make a well in the centre of the dry ingredients. Pour in the lukewarm water and the saffron liquid and start to mix together a little.

3 Add the oil and basil and continue to mix to form a soft dough, then transfer to a lightly floured surface and knead for about 10 minutes, or until the dough is smooth and elastic.

4 Place in a greased bowl, cover with clear film and leave to rise in a warm place for about 1 hour, or until the dough has doubled in bulk.

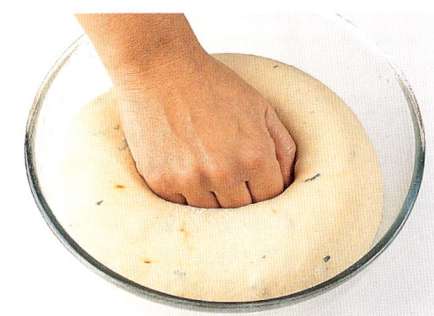

5 Knock back (punch down) the dough and transfer it to a lightly floured surface. Knead it for 2–3 minutes.

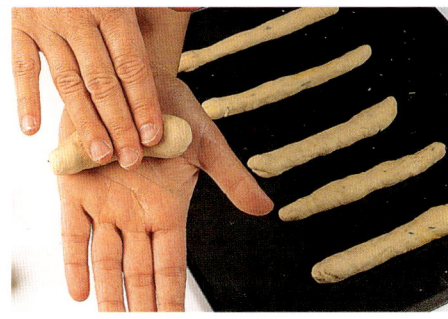

6 Preheat the oven to 220°C/425°F/Gas 7. Lightly grease two baking sheets and set aside. Divide the dough into 32 even pieces and shape into long sticks. Place them well apart on the prepared baking sheets, then leave them for a further 15–20 minutes, or until they become puffy. Bake in the oven for about 15 minutes, or until crisp and golden. Transfer to a wire rack to cool. Serve warm or cold.

OLIVE AND OREGANO BREAD

THIS TASTY ITALIAN BREAD IS HIGHLY FLAVOURED WITH OREGANO, PARSLEY AND OLIVES AND IS AN EXCELLENT ACCOMPANIMENT TO ALL SALADS. SERVE WARM TO ENJOY THE FLAVOURS AT THEIR BEST.

MAKES ONE LOAF

INGREDIENTS

7g/¼oz fresh yeast or 5ml/1 tsp
  dried yeast
pinch of sugar
300ml/½ pint/1¼ cups warm water
15ml/1 tbsp olive oil, plus extra
  for greasing
1 onion, chopped
450g/1lb/4 cups strong white bread
  flour, plus extra for dusting
5ml/1 tsp salt
1.5ml/¼ tsp ground black pepper
50g/2oz/½ cup pitted black olives,
  roughly chopped
15ml/1 tbsp black olive paste
15ml/1 tbsp chopped fresh oregano
15ml/1 tbsp chopped fresh parsley

1 Cream the fresh yeast with the sugar, and then gradually stir in half the warm water. If you are using dried yeast, put half the warm water in a jug (pitcher) and then sprinkle the yeast on top.

2 Add the sugar, stir well and leave the mixture to stand for 10 minutes, or until it is frothy.

3 Heat the oil in a frying pan and fry the onion until golden brown, stirring occasionally. Remove the pan from the heat and set aside.

4 Sift the flour into a mixing bowl with the salt and pepper. Make a well in the centre. Add the yeast mixture, the fried onions (with the oil), the olives, olive paste, oregano, parsley and remaining water. Gradually incorporate the flour, and mix to a soft dough, adding a little extra water if necessary.

5 Turn the dough out on to a lightly floured surface and knead for 5 minutes, or until smooth and elastic.

6 Place in a mixing bowl, cover with a damp dish towel and leave to rise in a warm place for about 2 hours until the dough has doubled in bulk. Lightly grease a baking sheet and set aside.

7 Turn the dough out on to a lightly floured surface and knead again for a few minutes. Shape into a 20cm/8in flat round and place on the prepared baking sheet.

8 Using a sharp knife, make criss-cross cuts over the top of the dough. Cover and leave in a warm place for 30 minutes, or until well risen. Preheat the oven to 220°C/425°F/Gas 7.

9 Dust the loaf with a little flour. Bake in the oven for 10 minutes then lower the oven temperature to 200°C/400°F/Gas 6. Bake for a further 20 minutes, or until the loaf sounds hollow when it is tapped underneath. Transfer to a wire rack to cool. Serve the bread warm or cold in slices or wedges.

WELSH CLAY-POT LOAVES WITH HERBS

THESE BREADS ARE FLAVOURED WITH CHIVES, PARSLEY, SAGE AND GARLIC, AND TOPPED WITH FENNEL SEEDS. YOU CAN USE ANY SELECTION OF YOUR FAVOURITE HERBS. FOR EVEN MORE FLAVOUR, TRY ADDING A LITTLE GRATED RAW ONION AND GRATED CHEESE TO THE DOUGH.

MAKES TWO LOAVES

INGREDIENTS

  50g/2oz/¼ cup butter, melted, plus
    extra for greasing
  115g/4oz/1 cup wholemeal (whole-
    wheat) bread flour
  350g/12oz/3 cups unbleached strong
    white bread flour, plus extra for dusting
  7.5ml/1½ tsp salt
  15g/½oz fresh yeast
  150ml/¼ pint/⅔ cup lukewarm milk
  120ml/4fl oz/½ cup lukewarm water
  15ml/1 tbsp chopped fresh chives
  15ml/1 tbsp chopped fresh parsley
  5ml/1 tsp chopped fresh sage
  1 garlic clove, crushed
  oil, for greasing
  beaten egg, for glazing
  fennel seeds, for sprinkling (optional)

1 Lightly grease two clean 14cm/5½in-diameter, 12cm/4½in-high clay flower pots. Sift the flours and salt together into a large bowl and make a well in the centre.

2 Blend the yeast with a little of the milk until smooth, then stir in the remaining milk. Pour the yeast liquid into the centre of the flour and sprinkle over a little of the flour from around the edge. Cover the bowl and leave in a warm place for 15 minutes.

3 Add the water, melted butter, herbs and garlic to the flour mixture and blend together to form a dough. Turn out on to a lightly floured surface and knead for about 10 minutes, or until the dough is smooth and elastic.

4 Place in a lightly oiled bowl, cover with lightly oiled clear film and leave to rise, in a warm place, for 1¼–1½ hours, or until doubled in bulk.

5 Turn the dough out on to a lightly floured surface and knock back (punch down). Divide in two. Shape and fit into the flower pots. It should about half fill the pots. Cover with oiled clear film and leave to rise for 30–45 minutes in a warm place, or until the dough is 2.5cm/1in from the top of the pots.

6 Meanwhile, preheat the oven to 200°C/400°F/Gas 6. Brush the tops with beaten egg and sprinkle with fennel seeds, if using. Bake for 35–40 minutes, or until golden. Turn out on to a wire rack to cool.

PAIN AUX NOIX

THIS DELICIOUS BUTTER AND MILK-ENRICHED BREAD IS FILLED WITH WALNUTS. IT IS THE PERFECT COMPANION FOR CHEESE.

MAKES TWO LOAVES

INGREDIENTS
50g/2oz/¼ cup butter
350g/12oz/3 cups wholemeal (whole-wheat) bread flour
15ml/1 tbsp light muscovado (brown) sugar
7.5ml/1½ tsp salt
20g/¾ oz fresh yeast
275ml/9fl oz/generous 1 cup lukewarm milk
175g/6oz/1½ cups walnut pieces

1 Lightly grease two baking sheets. Place the butter in a small pan and heat until melted and starting to turn brown, then set aside to cool. Mix the flour, sugar and salt in a large bowl and make a well in the centre. Cream the yeast with half the milk. Add to the centre of the flour with the remaining milk.

2 Pour the cool melted butter through a fine strainer into the liquids in the centre of the flour. Using your hand, mix the ingredients together in the bowl and gradually mix in small quantities of the flour to make batter. Continue until the mixture forms a moist dough.

3 Knead on a lightly floured surface for 6–8 minutes. Place in a lightly oiled bowl, cover with lightly oiled clear film and leave to rise, in a warm place, for 1 hour, or until doubled in bulk.

4 Turn out on to a lightly floured surface and gently knock back (punch down). Press or roll to flatten and then sprinkle over the nuts. Gently press the nuts into the dough, then roll it up. Return to the oiled bowl, re-cover and leave, in a warm place, for 30 minutes.

5 Turn out on to a lightly floured surface, divide in half and shape each piece into a ball. Place on the baking sheets, cover with lightly oiled clear film and leave to rise, in a warm place, for 45 minutes, or until doubled in bulk.

6 Meanwhile, preheat the oven to 220°C/425°F/Gas 7. Using a sharp knife, slash the top of each loaf three times. Bake for 35 minutes, or until the loaves sound hollow when tapped on the base. Transfer to a wire rack to cool.

LAVENDER SCONES

LEND AN UNUSUAL BUT DELICIOUS LAVENDER PERFUME TO YOUR SCONES — ITS FRAGRANCE MARRIES WELL WITH THE SWEETNESS OF SUMMER SOFT FRUIT AND MAKES FOR AN ELEGANT TEA-TIME TREAT. THE LAVENDER'S SCENTED QUALITY GIVES THE WELL-KNOWN TEA SCONE A FLAVOUR, WHICH NOWADAYS CAN SEEM PLEASANTLY UNUSUAL AND SURPRISING.

MAKES TWELVE

INGREDIENTS

   225g/8oz/2 cups plain (all-purpose)
     flour, plus extra for dusting
   15ml/1 tbsp baking powder
   50g/2oz/¼ cup butter
   50g/2oz/¼ cup sugar
   10ml/2 tsp fresh lavender florets or
     5ml/1 tsp dried culinary lavender,
     roughly chopped
   about 150ml/¼ pint/⅔ cup milk
   plum jam and clotted cream, to serve

1 Preheat the oven to 220°C/425°F/ Gas 7. Sift the flour and baking powder together. Rub the butter into the flour mixture until it resembles fine breadcrumbs.

2 Stir in the sugar and chopped lavender, reserving a pinch to sprinkle on the top of the scones (US biscuits) before baking them. Add enough milk so that the mixture forms a soft, sticky dough. Bind the dough together and then turn it out on to a floured surface.

3 Shape the dough into a round, gently patting down the top to give a 2.5cm/ 1in depth. Using a floured cutter, stamp out 12 scones.

4 Place the scones on a baking sheet. Brush the tops with a little milk and sprinkle over the reserved lavender.

5 Bake the scones for 10–12 minutes, or until golden. Serve warm with plum jam and clotted cream.

LAVENDER CAKE

BAKE A SUMMER-SCENTED CAKE THAT IS REMINISCENT OF THOSE DISTANT ELIZABETHAN TIMES WHEN LAVENDER WAS AN EXTREMELY POPULAR CULINARY HERB, NOT JUST FOR ITS EVOCATIVE FRAGRANCE BUT FOR ITS DISTINCTIVE FLAVOUR, TOO.

SERVES EIGHT

INGREDIENTS

175g/6oz/¾ cup unsalted (sweet) butter, plus extra for greasing
175g/6oz/scant 1 cup caster (superfine) sugar
3 eggs, lightly beaten
175g/6oz/1⅔ cups self-raising (self-rising) flour, sifted, plus extra
30ml/2 tbsp fresh lavender florets
2.5ml/½ tsp vanilla essence (extract)
30ml/2 tbsp milk
50g/2oz/½ cup icing (confectioners') sugar, sifted
2.5ml/½ tsp water
a few fresh lavender florets

1 Preheat the oven to 180°C/350°F/ Gas 4. Lightly grease and flour a ring tin (pan) or a deep 20cm/8in round, loose-based cake tin (pan).

2 Cream the butter and sugar together thoroughly until the mixture is light and fluffy.

3 Add the beaten egg gradually, beating thoroughly between each separate addition, until the mixture has become thick and glossy.

4 Gently fold in the flour, together with the lavender florets, vanilla essence and milk.

5 Spoon the mixture into the tin and bake for 1 hour. Leave to stand for 5 minutes, then turn out on to a wire rack to cool.

6 Mix the icing sugar with the water until smooth. Pour the icing over the cake and decorate with a few fresh lavender florets.

VARIATION
For a pretty colour contrast, add a little orange food colouring to the icing before pouring over the cake.

LAVENDER HEART COOKIES

IN FOLKLORE, LAVENDER HAS ALWAYS BEEN LINKED WITH LOVE, AS HAS FOOD. SO MAKE SOME OF THESE HEART-SHAPED COOKIES AND SERVE THEM TO YOUR LOVED ONE ON VALENTINE'S DAY, OR ON ANY OTHER ROMANTIC ANNIVERSARY.

MAKES SIXTEEN TO EIGHTEEN

INGREDIENTS

    115g/4oz/½ cup unsalted (sweet) butter, softened
    50g/2oz/¼ cup caster (superfine) sugar
    175g/6oz/1½ cups plain (all-purpose) flour, plus extra for dusting
    30ml/2 tbsp fresh lavender florets or 15ml/1 tbsp dried culinary lavender, roughly chopped
    25g/1oz/¼ cup icing (confectioners') sugar, for sprinkling

1 Cream the butter and sugar together until light and fluffy.

2 Mix together the flour and lavender, and add to the creamed mixture. Bring the mixture together in a soft ball. Cover and chill for 15 minutes.

3 Preheat the oven to 200°C/400°F/ Gas 6. Roll out the mixture on a lightly floured surface and stamp out about 18 biscuits (cookies), using a 5cm/2in heart-shaped cutter.

4 Place the biscuits on a heavy baking sheet and bake for about 10 minutes until they are golden.

5 Leave the biscuits to stand for about 5 minutes to firm up, then, using a palette knife (metal spatula), transfer them carefully from the baking sheet on to a wire rack to cool completely.

6 Sprinkle with icing sugar. You can store the biscuits in an airtight container for up to 1 week.

COOK'S TIPS
• Metal cutters make cutting easier, but remember to ensure that they are completely dry before putting them away, or they will turn rusty.
• Biscuits such as these can be made in advance and frozen very successfully, as long as they are well wrapped.

LEMON AND WALNUT CAKE

DON'T STINT ON THE LEMON RIND — IT GIVES THIS CAKE A WONDERFUL ZESTY TANG THAT BLENDS PERFECTLY WITH THE WARM FLAVOUR OF THE WALNUTS.

4 Scrape the mixture into a bowl and fold in the remaining flour, with the walnut pieces.

5 Grate (shred) the rind from three lemons and thinly pare the rind from the fourth (reserve for the decoration). Squeeze the juice from two lemons, then stir the grated lemon rind and juice into the cake mixture.

6 Spoon the mixture into the prepared tin. Bake for 50–60 minutes, or until a fine skewer inserted in the centre of the cake comes out clean. Cool on a wire rack. Decorate the cake with the pared lemon rind.

COOK'S TIPS
• If the dried dates are very hard, soften them in boiling water for 10 minutes before draining and using.
• Make sure that you buy plain dried dates and not the kind that are chopped and coated with sugar.
• Look out for packets of walnut pieces in supermarkets, as they are usually much less expensive than either shelled walnuts or walnut halves.

SERVES EIGHT TO TEN

INGREDIENTS
    1 large banana, about 150g/5oz
    225g/8oz/1 cup butter, plus extra
      for greasing
    150g/5oz/1 cup dried, pitted
      dates, chopped
    5 small (US medium) eggs
    300g/11oz/scant 3 cups wholemeal
      (whole-wheat) flour, or half
      wholemeal and half plain (all-
      purpose) white flour
    75g/3oz/¾ cup walnut pieces
    4 large lemons

1 Preheat the oven to 180°C/350°F/ Gas 4. Grease a deep 20cm/8in spring-form cake tin (pan). Line the base of the tin with baking parchment.

2 Peel and chop the banana. Process with the butter and dates in a food processor or blender.

3 Add one egg and 15ml/1 tbsp of the flour to the creamed mixture. Process briefly to mix, then add the remaining eggs one at a time, each with a further 15ml/1 tbsp flour.

SUNFLOWER SULTANA SCONES

THESE FRUITY SCONES HAVE A TASTY SUNFLOWER-SEED TOPPING. THEY MAKE A TEMPTING TEA-TIME TREAT SPREAD WITH BUTTER AND JAM.

MAKES TEN TO TWELVE

INGREDIENTS
  oil, for greasing
  225g/8oz/2 cups self-raising (self-
    rising) flour, plus extra for dusting
  5ml/1 tsp baking powder
  25g/1oz/2 tbsp butter
  30ml/2 tbsp golden caster (superfine)
    sugar
  50g/2oz/⅓ cup sultanas (golden raisins)
  30ml/2 tbsp sunflower seeds
  150g/5oz/⅔ cup natural (plain) yogurt
  about 30–45ml/2–3 tbsp skimmed
    (low-fat) milk
  butter and jam, to serve (optional)

1 Preheat the oven to 230ºC/450ºF/
Gas 8. Lightly oil a baking sheet. Sift
the flour and baking powder into a bowl
and rub in the butter.

2 Stir in the sugar, sultanas and half the
sunflower seeds, then mix in the yogurt,
with just enough milk to make a fairly
soft, but not sticky dough.

3 Roll out on a lightly floured surface to
a thickness of about 2cm/¾in. Cut into
6cm/2½in rounds with a biscuit (cookie)
cutter and lift on to the baking sheet.

4 Brush the scones (US biscuits) with
milk and then sprinkle with the reserved
sunflower seeds. Bake in the preheated
oven for 10–12 minutes, or until they
are well risen and golden brown.

5 Cool the scones on a wire rack. Serve
them split and spread with butter and
jam, if you like.

TREACLE, DATE AND WALNUT CAKE

LAYERED WITH DATE PURÉE AND FINISHED WITH A CRUNCHY SUGAR AND WALNUT TOPPING, THIS CAKE IS ABSOLUTELY IRRESISTIBLE.

MAKES ONE CAKE

INGREDIENTS

140g/5oz/scant 1 cup pitted dates
grated rind and juice of 1 lemon
170g/6oz/1½ cups self-raising
  (self-rising) flour
3.5ml/¾ tsp each ground cinnamon,
  ginger and grated nutmeg
75g/3oz/6 tbsp light muscovado
  (brown) sugar
22ml/1½ tbsp treacle (molasses)
45ml/3 tbsp golden (light corn) syrup
60ml/4 tbsp milk
1 large (US extra large) egg
50g/2oz/½ cup chopped walnuts
For the topping
25g/1oz/2 tbsp butter
50g/2oz/¼ cup light muscovado
  (brown) sugar
22ml/1½ tbsp plain (all-purpose) flour
3.5ml/¾ tsp ground cinnamon
40g/1½oz/⅓ cup chopped walnuts

1 Set the oven to 180°C/350°F/ Gas 4. Line a 500g/1¼lb loaf tin (pan) with baking parchment or greased greaseproof paper. Mix the dates, lemon rind and lemon juice in a pan. Add 60ml/4 tbsp of water and bring to the boil, then simmer until soft. Purée in a blender or food processor until smooth.

2 Sift the flour and spices together. Cream the butter and sugar until pale and fluffy. Warm the treacle, golden sryup and milk in a pan, until just melted, then beat into the creamed butter mixture. Add the egg and beat in the flour mixture. Stir in the walnuts.

3 Place half the mixture in the loaf tin. Spread over the date purée, leaving a narrow border of cake mix all round. Top with the remaining cake mixture, spreading it evenly over the date purée.

4 Bake the cake for 40 minutes or until golden brown.

5 Mix all of the topping ingredients together. When the cake has baked for the recommended time, sprinkle the topping over and cook for 10–15 minutes more, until the topping starts to bubble and the cake is cooked. Remove the loaf tin from the oven. Leave to stand for 10 minutes, then turn out on to a wire rack to cool.

desserts,
ices & sorbets

Herbs are perhaps least known for the wonderful lift they give to

desserts and ices. The delicate scent of rose petals can define a buttery

raspberry shortcake, subtle apple snow or refreshing summer sorbet.

For an exotic barbecue, thread lemon grass "skewers" with chunks of

fruit so the aromatic, lemon flavour permeates through. Try a memorable

decoration for a creamy pavlova or elegant gâteau with freshly picked

garden herb flowers. Even herbs like rosemary and bay make an

inspired addition to the smoothest, creamiest and best

home-made ice cream.

RASPBERRY AND ROSE-PETAL SHORTCAKES

ROSE-WATER-SCENTED CREAM AND FRESH RASPBERRIES FORM THE FILLING FOR THIS DELECTABLE AND LUXURIOUS DESSERT. ALTHOUGH THEY LOOK IMPRESSIVE, THESE SHORTCAKES ARE EASY TO MAKE AND WOULD BE AN EXCELLENT CHOICE FOR A DINNER PARTY.

MAKES SIX

INGREDIENTS
   115g/4oz/½ cup unsalted (sweet)
      butter, softened
   50g/2oz/¼ cup caster (superfine)
      sugar
   ½ vanilla pod (bean), split and
      seeds reserved
   115g/4oz/1 cup plain (all-purpose)
      flour, plus extra for dusting
   50g/2oz/⅓ cup semolina
For the filling
   300ml/½ pint/1¼ cups double
      (heavy) cream
   15ml/1 tbsp icing (confectioners')
      sugar, plus extra for dusting
   2.5ml/½ tsp rose water
   450g/1lb/2⅔ cups raspberries
For the decoration
   12 miniature roses, unsprayed
   6 mint sprigs
   1 egg white, beaten
   caster (superfine) sugar, for dusting

1 Cream the butter, sugar and vanilla seeds together in a bowl until the mixture is pale and fluffy. Sift the flour and semolina together, then gradually work the dry ingredients into the creamed mixture to make a biscuit (cookie) dough.

VARIATIONS
Other soft, red summer berries, such as mulberries, loganberries and tayberries, would be equally good in this dessert. You might also like to use different shapes of cutter for the shortcakes, such as flowers and hearts.

2 Gently knead the dough on a lightly floured surface until smooth. Roll out quite thinly and prick all over with a fork. Using a 7.5cm/3in fluted cutter, cut out 12 rounds. Place these on a baking sheet and then chill in the refrigerator for 30 minutes.

3 Meanwhile, make the filling. Whisk the double cream with the icing sugar until soft peaks form. Gently fold the rose water into the mixture and then chill until required.

4 Preheat the oven to 180°C/350°F/ Gas 4. Paint the roses and mint sprigs with the beaten egg white. Dust with sugar; place on a wire rack to dry.

5 Bake the shortcakes in the preheated oven for 15 minutes, or until they are lightly golden. Lift them off the baking sheet with a metal fish slice (spatula) and transfer to a wire rack to cool.

6 To assemble the shortcakes, spoon the rose-water cream on to half the shortcakes. Arrange a layer of raspberries on top of the cream, then top with a second shortcake.

7 Dust the filled shortcakes with icing sugar. Decorate with the frosted roses and mint sprigs.

COOK'S TIPS
• For best results, serve the shortcakes as soon as possible after assembling them. Otherwise, they are likely to turn soggy from the raspberries' liquid.
• If necessary, ground rice can be substituted for the semolina used for making the shortcakes.
• For the best-flavoured shortcakes, always use butter and not margarine.

APPLE AND ROSE-PETAL SNOW

THIS IS A LOVELY, LIGHT AND REFRESHING DESSERT, WHICH IS IDEAL TO MAKE WHEN THE ORCHARDS ARE GROANING WITH APPLES. THE ROSE PETALS GIVE A DELICATE FRAGRANCE BUT OTHER EDIBLE PETALS SUCH AS HONEYSUCKLE, LAVENDER AND GERANIUM COULD ALSO BE USED.

SERVES FOUR

INGREDIENTS

2 large cooking apples
150ml/¼ pint/⅔ cup thick
   apple juice
30ml/2 tbsp rose water
2 egg whites
75g/3oz/6 tbsp caster (superfine) sugar
a few rose petals from an
   unsprayed rose
crystallized rose petals, to decorate
crisp biscuits (cookies) or brandy
   snaps, to serve

VARIATION
Make an Apple and Rose-petal Fool. Fold 150ml¼ pint/⅔ cup each custard and whipped cream into the apple purée.

1 Peel and chop the apples and cook them with the apple juice until they are soft. Sieve, add the rose water and leave to cool.

2 Whisk the egg whites until they form stiff peaks, then gently whisk in the caster sugar.

3 Gently fold together the apple and rose water purée and the egg whites. Stir in most of the rose petals.

4 Spoon the snow into four glasses and chill. Decorate with the crystallized rose petals and serve with some crisp biscuits or brandy snaps.

BANANAS <u>WITH</u> LIME <u>AND</u> CARDAMOM SAUCE

AROMATIC CARDAMOM AND FRESH LIME GIVE AN EXOTIC HINT TO THE FLAKED ALMONDS IN THIS DELICIOUS SAUCE FOR POURING OVER BANANAS.

SERVES FOUR

INGREDIENTS
  6 small bananas
  50g/2oz/¼ cup butter
  50g/2oz/½ cup flaked (sliced) almonds
  seeds from 4 cardamom
   pods, crushed
  thinly pared rind and juice
   of 2 limes
  50g/2oz/¼ cup light muscovado
   (brown) sugar
  30ml/2 tbsp dark rum
  vanilla ice cream, to serve

VARIATIONS
If you prefer not to use alcohol in your cooking, replace the rum with a fruit juice of your choice, such as orange or even pineapple juice. The sauce is equally good poured over folded crêpes.

1 Peel the bananas and cut them in half lengthways. Heat half the butter in a large frying pan. Add half the bananas, and cook until the undersides are golden. Turn carefully, using a fish slice (spatula). Cook until golden.

2 As they cook, transfer the bananas to a heatproof serving dish. Cook the remaining bananas in the same way.

3 Melt the remaining butter, then add the almonds and cardamom seeds. Cook, stirring until golden.

4 Stir in the lime rind and juice, then the sugar. Cook, stirring, until the mixture is smooth, bubbling and slightly reduced. Stir in the rum. Pour the sauce over the bananas and serve immediately, with vanilla ice cream.

WALNUT SHORTBREAD WITH SPICED APPLE SLICES

SOFT, CARAMELIZED APPLES WITH GINGER, CINNAMON AND NUTMEG MAKE A PERFECT ACCOMPANIMENT FOR WALNUT SHORTBREAD. SERVE WARM WITH YOGURT OR ICE CREAM.

SERVES FOUR

INGREDIENTS

- 25g/1oz/2 tbsp unsalted (sweet) butter
- 4 dessert apples, thinly sliced
- 30ml/2 tbsp soft light brown sugar
- 10ml/2 tsp ground ginger
- 5ml/1 tsp ground cinnamon
- 2.5ml/½ tsp ground nutmeg

For the walnut shortbread

- 75g/3oz/⅔ cup wholemeal (whole-wheat) flour
- 75g/3oz/⅔ cup unbleached plain (all-purpose) flour, plus extra for dusting
- 25g/1oz/¼ cup oatmeal
- 5ml/1 tsp baking powder
- 1.5ml/¼ tsp salt
- 50g/2oz/¼ cup golden caster (superfine) sugar
- 115g/4oz/½ cup unsalted (sweet) butter, plus extra for greasing
- 40g/1½oz/¼ cup walnuts, finely chopped
- 15ml/1 tbsp milk, plus extra for brushing
- demerara (raw) sugar, for sprinkling

1 Preheat the oven to 180°C/350°F/Gas 4. Grease one or two baking sheets.

2 To make the walnut shortbread, sift together the flours, adding any bran left in the sieve, and mix with the oatmeal, baking powder, salt and sugar. Rub in the butter with your fingers until the mixture resembles fine breadcrumbs.

3 Add the chopped walnuts, then stir in enough of the milk to form a soft dough.

4 Gently knead the dough on a floured work surface. Form into a round, then roll out to a 5mm/¼in thickness. Using a 7.5cm/3in fluted cutter, stamp out eight rounds – you may have some dough left over.

5 Place the shortbread rounds on the prepared baking sheets. Brush the tops with milk and sprinkle with sugar. Bake for 12–15 minutes, or until golden, then transfer to a wire rack and leave to cool.

6 To prepare the apples, melt the butter in a heavy frying pan. Add the apple slices and cook for 3–4 minutes over a gentle heat until softened.

7 Increase the heat to medium, add the sugar and spices, and stir well. Cook for a few minutes, stirring frequently, until the sauce turns golden brown and caramelizes. Serve warm, with the shortbread.

GARDEN FLOWER PAVLOVA

PAVLOVA MUST BE ONE OF THE MOST LAVISH DESSERTS. HERE IT IS PERFUMED WITH LAVENDER SUGAR, FILLED WITH FRESH PEACHES AND CREAM, AND DECORATED WITH SUGARED FLOWERS. IT MAKES AN ENCHANTING SUMMER TREAT.

SERVES EIGHT

INGREDIENTS
   5 large egg whites
   250g/9oz/1¼ cups lavender sugar
   5ml/1 tsp cornflour (cornstarch)
   5ml/1 tsp white wine vinegar
   sugared flowers, to decorate
For the filling
   300ml/½ pint/1¼ cups double
      (heavy) cream
   2 ripe peaches

COOK'S TIP
To make lavender sugar, mix 15ml/1 tbsp dried culinary lavender with 1kg/2¼lb/5 cups caster (superfine) sugar. Store in an airtight container. Shake regularly.

1 Preheat the oven to 110°C/225°F/Gas ¼. Line two baking sheets with baking parchment and draw a 23cm/9in circle on one and a 16cm/6¼in circle on the second.

2 Put the egg whites in a large bowl and whisk until they form stiff but moist-looking peaks. Gradually whisk in the sugar, a spoonful at a time, and continue whisking for 2 minutes until the meringue is thick and glossy.

3 Mix the cornflour and vinegar together and fold into the meringue mixture. Using two dessertspoons, drop spoonfuls of meringue over the smaller circle. Make the larger circle in the same way, and level the centre slightly.

4 Cook for 1¼ hours, or until pale golden. (Swap the positions of the baking sheets during cooking so that the layers cook to an even colour.) The meringues should come away from the paper easily; test by peeling away an edge of the paper but leave the meringues on the paper to cool.

5 To serve, remove the paper and put the larger meringue on a large, flat serving plate. Softly whip the cream, and spoon over the meringue. Halve, stone and slice the peaches and arrange on the cream. Place the second meringue on top of the peaches. Chill. When ready to serve, decorate with a selection of crystallized flowers and serve immediately.

MAPLE AND WALNUT MERINGUE GATEAU

RICH WALNUTS AND SWEET MAPLE SYRUP ARE GREAT PARTNERS AND GO PARTICULARLY WELL WITH PALE-GOLDEN MERINGUE. THIS ICED DESSERT IS A FEAST FOR ALL MERINGUE LOVERS.

SERVES TEN TO TWELVE

INGREDIENTS
  4 egg whites
  200g/7oz/scant 1 cup light
    muscovado (brown) sugar
  150g/5oz/1¼ cups walnut pieces
  600ml/1 pint/2½ cups double
    (heavy) cream
  150ml/¼ pint/⅔ cup maple syrup,
    plus extra, to serve

1 Preheat the oven to 140°C/275°F/ Gas 1. Draw three 23cm/9in circles on separate sheets of non-stick baking parchment. Invert the sheets on three baking sheets. Whisk the egg whites in a grease-free bowl until stiff.

2 Whisk in the sugar, about 15ml/1 tbsp at a time, whisking well after each addition until the meringue is stiff and glossy. Spread to within 1cm/½in of the edge of each marked circle. Bake for about 1 hour or until crisp, swapping the baking sheets around halfway through cooking. Leave to cool.

3 Set aside 45ml/3 tbsp of the walnuts. Finely chop the remainder. Whip the cream with the maple syrup until it forms soft peaks. Fold in the chopped walnuts. Use about a third of the mixture to sandwich the meringues together on a flat, freezerproof serving plate.

4 Using a palette knife (metal spatula), spread the remaining cream mixture over the top and sides of the gâteau. Sprinkle with the reserved walnuts and freeze overnight.

5 Transfer the gâteau to the refrigerator about 1 hour before serving so that the cream filling softens slightly. Drizzle over the top a little of the extra maple syrup, just before serving. Serve in slices.

LEMON GRASS SKEWERS <u>WITH</u> LIME CHEESE

GRILLED FRUITS MAKE A FINE FINALE TO A BARBECUE, WHETHER THEY ARE COOKED OVER THE COALS OR UNDER A HOT GRILL. THE LEMON GRASS SKEWERS GIVE THE FRUIT A SUBTLE LEMON TANG. THE FRUITS USED HERE MAKE AN IDEAL EXOTIC MIX, BUT ALMOST ANY SOFT FRUIT CAN BE SUBSTITUTED.

SERVES FOUR

INGREDIENTS
1 mango
1 papaya
1 star fruit
4 long fresh lemon grass stalks
8 fresh bay leaves
freshly grated nutmeg
60ml/4 tbsp maple syrup
50g/2oz/⅓ cup demerara (raw) sugar
For the lime cheese
150g/5oz/⅔ cup curd cheese or low
  fat soft (white farmer's) cheese
120ml/4fl oz/½ cup double
  (heavy) cream
grated rind and juice of ½ lime
30ml/2 tbsp icing (confectioners')
  sugar

1 Prepare the fruit. Peel, stone (pit) or seed, and cut the mango and papaya into chunks. Halve the star fruit and cut into thick slices.

2 Prepare the barbecue or preheat the grill (broiler). Cut the top of each lemon grass stalk into a point with a sharp knife. Discard the outer leaves, then use the back of the knife to bruise the length of each stalk to release the aromatic oils. Thread each stalk, skewer-style, with the fruit pieces and bay leaves.

3 Place a piece of foil on a baking sheet. Roll up the edges to make a rim. Grease the foil, add the kebabs and grate nutmeg over each. Drizzle the syrup over and dust with the demerara sugar. Grill (broil) for 5 minutes, until lightly charred.

4 Meanwhile, make the lime cheese. Mix together the cheese, cream, grated lime rind and juice and icing sugar in a bowl. Serve immediately with the lightly charred fruit kebabs.

COOK'S TIP
Only fresh lemon grass will work as skewers for this recipe. It is now possible to buy lemon grass stalks in jars.

MINT ICE CREAM

THIS REFRESHING AND INVIGORATING FRESH MINT ICE CREAM WILL BE DELICIOUSLY COOLING ON A HOT SUMMER'S DAY.

SERVES EIGHT

INGREDIENTS
    8 egg yolks
    75g/3oz/6 tbsp caster (superfine) sugar
    600ml/1 pint/2½ cups single (light) cream
    1 vanilla pod (bean)
    60ml/4 tbsp chopped fresh mint
    mint sprigs, to decorate

1 Beat the egg yolks and sugar until pale and light. Transfer to a small pan.

2 In a separate pan, bring the cream to the boil with the vanilla pod.

3 Remove the vanilla pod and pour on to the egg mixture, whisking briskly.

4 Continue whisking to ensure the eggs are mixed into the cream, then gently heat the mixture until the custard thickens enough to coat the back of a wooden spoon. Leave to cool.

5 By hand: Stir in the mint, then transfer to a freezerproof container. Freeze until the mixture is mushy then beat using a fork, a whisk or a food processor to break up the ice crystals. Freeze for another 3 hours, or until it is softly frozen, then whisk again. Finally, freeze until the ice cream is firm (this will take at least 6 hours).

Using an ice cream maker: Stir in the mint and churn in an ice cream maker until firm.

6 Transfer to the refrigerator for 20 minutes before serving, so that it will soften a little. Decorate with mint sprigs.

STRAWBERRY AND LAVENDER SORBET

DELICATELY PERFUMED WITH JUST A HINT OF LAVENDER, THIS DELIGHTFUL, PASTEL PINK SORBET IS PERFECT FOR A SPECIAL-OCCASION DINNER.

SERVES SIX

INGREDIENTS
   150g/5oz/¾ cup caster (superfine)
      sugar
   300ml/½ pint/1¼ cups water
   6 fresh lavender flowers
   500g/1¼lb/5 cups strawberries,
      hulled
   1 egg white
   lavender flowers, to decorate

1 Put the sugar and measured water into a pan and bring to the boil, stirring constantly until the sugar has completely dissolved.

2 Take the pan off the heat, add the lavender flowers and leave to infuse (steep) for 1 hour. If time permits, chill the syrup before using.

3 Purée the strawberries in a food processor or in batches in a blender, then press the purée (paste) through a large sieve into a bowl.

4 By hand: Spoon the purée into a plastic tub or similar freezerproof container, strain in the lavender syrup and freeze for 4 hours, or until the mixture is mushy.
Using an ice cream maker: Pour the strawberry purée into the bowl of an ice cream maker and strain in the lavender syrup. Churn for 20 minutes, or until the mixture is thick.

5 Whisk the egg white until it has just turned frothy.
By hand: Scoop the sorbet from the tub into a food processor, process it until smooth, then add the egg white. Spoon the sorbet back into the tub and freeze for 4 hours, or until firm.
Using an ice cream maker: Add the egg white to the ice cream maker and continue to churn until the sorbet is firm enough to scoop.

6 Serve the sorbet in scoops, decorated with lavender flowers.

COOK'S TIP
The size of the lavender flowers may vary; if they are very small you may need to use eight instead of six. To double check, taste a little of the cooled lavender syrup. If you think the flavour is a little mild, add 2–3 more flowers, reheat and cool again before using.

KULFI WITH CARDAMOM

THIS FAMOUS INDIAN ICE CREAM IS TRADITIONALLY MADE BY SLOWLY BOILING MILK UNTIL IT HAS REDUCED TO ABOUT ONE-THIRD OF THE ORIGINAL QUANTITY. CARDAMOMS ARE SIMMERED WITH THE MILK SO THAT IT IS INFUSED WITH THEIR DELICATE, SPICY FLAVOUR.

SERVES FOUR

INGREDIENTS

1.5 litres/2½ pints/6¼ cups full-fat (whole) milk
3 cardamom pods
25g/1oz/2 tbsp caster (superfine) sugar
50g/2oz/⅓ cup pistachio nuts, skinned
a few pink rose petals from an unsprayed rose, to decorate

1 Pour the milk into a large pan. Bring to the boil, lower the heat and simmer gently for 1 hour, stirring occasionally.

2 Put the cardamom pods in a mortar and crush them with a pestle. Add the pods and the seeds to the hot milk in the pan and continue to simmer the milk for 1–1½ hours, or until the volume of milk has reduced to about 475ml/ 16fl oz/2 cups.

3 Strain the flavoured milk into a jug (pitcher) or bowl, stir in the caster sugar and then leave to cool.

4 Grind half the skinned pistachio nuts to a smooth powder in a blender, nut grinder or cleaned coffee grinder. Cut the remaining nuts into thin slivers and set them aside for the decoration. Stir the ground pistachio nuts into the milk mixture.

5 Pour the milk mixture into four kulfi moulds. Freeze overnight until the kulfi is firm.

6 To unmould the kulfi, half-fill a plastic container or bowl with very hot water, stand the moulds in the water and count to ten. Immediately lift out the moulds and invert them on a baking sheet.

7 Transfer the ice creams to a platter or individual plates, cut a cross in the top of each and strew the sliced pistachios and rose petals around. Serve at once.

COOK'S TIPS

• Stay in the kitchen while the milk is simmering, so that you can control the heat to keep the milk gently bubbling without boiling over.

• If you don't have any kulfi moulds, use lolly moulds without the tops or even disposable plastic cups. If the ices won't turn out, dip a cloth in very hot water, wring it out and place it on the tops of the moulds, or plunge the moulds back into hot water for a few seconds.

ROSEMARY ICE CREAM

FRESH ROSEMARY HAS A LOVELY FRAGRANCE THAT WORKS AS WELL IN SWEET DISHES AS IT DOES IN SAVOURY. SERVE THIS ICE CREAM AS AN ACCOMPANIMENT TO SOFT FRUIT OR PLUM COMPOTE, OR ON ITS OWN, WITH AMARETTI OR RATAFIA BISCUITS.

2 Remove the rosemary sprigs from the milk, then return the pan to the heat and bring the milk almost to the boil. Pour it over the egg yolk mixture in the bowl, stirring well.

3 Return the mixture to the pan and cook it over a very gentle heat, stirring constantly until the custard thickens. Do not let it boil or the mixture may curdle.

4 Strain the custard through a sieve into a bowl. Cover the surface closely with greaseproof (waxed) paper and leave to cool. Chill until very cold, then stir in the crème fraîche.

5 By hand: Pour the mixture into a freezerproof container. Freeze for about 6 hours, beating twice using a fork, a whisk or a food processor to break up the ice crystals. Freeze until firm.
Using an ice cream maker: Churn the mixture in an ice cream maker until it is thick, then scrape it into a tub or similar freezerproof container. Freeze until ready to serve.

6 Transfer the ice cream to the refrigerator 30 minutes before serving so that it softens. Scoop into dessert dishes, sprinkle lightly with demerara sugar and decorate with rosemary sprigs and herb flowers. Offer amaretti or ratafia biscuits, if you like.

COOK'S TIP
A mixture of rosemary, lavender and chive flowers would look very attractive for the decoration.

SERVES SIX

INGREDIENTS
  300ml/½ pint/1¼ cups milk
  4 large fresh rosemary sprigs
  3 egg yolks
  75g/3oz/6 tbsp caster (superfine)
    sugar
  10ml/2 tsp cornflour (cornstarch)
  400ml/14fl oz/1⅔ cups crème fraîche
  about 15ml/1 tbsp demerara (raw)
    sugar
  fresh rosemary sprigs and herb
    flowers, to decorate
  amaretti or ratafia biscuits (almond
    macaroons), to serve (optional)

1 Put the milk and rosemary sprigs in a heavy pan. Bring almost to the boil, then remove from the heat and leave to infuse (steep) for 20 minutes. Whisk the egg yolks in a bowl with the sugar and cornflour.

ROSE-PETAL SORBET DECORATED WITH SUGARED ROSE PETALS

THIS SORBET MAKES A WONDERFUL END TO A SUMMER MEAL WITH ITS FABULOUS FLAVOUR OF ROSES. REMEMBER TO USE THE MOST SCENTED VARIETY YOU CAN FIND IN THE GARDEN. PICK FRESH BLOOMS WHICH ARE NEWLY OPENED, IDEALLY IN THE LATE MORNING, BEFORE THE HEAT OF THE DAY EVAPORATES THE ESSENTIAL OILS.

SERVES FOUR TO SIX

INGREDIENTS

115g/4oz/generous ½ cup caster (superfine) sugar
300ml/½ pint/1¼ cups boiling water
petals of 3 large, scented red or deep-pink roses from an unsprayed rose, white ends of petals removed
juice of 2 lemons
300ml/½ pint/1¼ cups rosé wine
whole crystallized roses or rose petals, to decorate

1 Place the sugar in a bowl and add the boiling water. Stir until the sugar has completely dissolved. Add the rose petals and leave to cool completely.

COOK'S TIPS
• If the sorbet is too hard, transfer it to the refrigerator for about 30 minutes before you are ready to serve.
• For a stunning presentation idea, scoop the sorbet into a rose ice bowl. The bowl and sorbet can be left in the freezer until they are needed.

2 Blend the mixture in a food processor, then strain through a sieve. Add the lemon juice and wine.

3 By hand: Pour into a freezerproof container. Freeze for several hours, or until ice crystals form around the edges. Whisk or use a food processor to break up the crystals. Re-freeze until frozen around the edges. Repeat the whisking and freezing process once or twice more, until the sorbet is pale and smooth. Freeze until firm.
Using an ice cream maker: Churn until firm with a good texture.

4 Serve in scoops, decorated with crystallized roses or rose petals.

VARIATION
If you prefer, a yellow version of this dish can be made using yellow rose petals and white wine instead of rosé.

ROSE GERANIUM MARQUISE

THIS DESSERT MAKES A GOOD CHOICE FOR A DINNER PARTY AS IT CAN BE MADE IN ADVANCE. ROSE GERANIUM LEAVES GIVE THE ICE CREAM A DELICATE, SCENTED FLAVOUR IN THIS ELEGANT DESSERT.

SERVES EIGHT

INGREDIENTS

225g/8oz/generous 1 cup caster (superfine) sugar
400ml/14fl oz/1⅔ cups water
24 fresh rose geranium leaves
45ml/3 tbsp lemon juice
250g/9oz/generous 1 cup mascarpone cheese
300ml/½ pint/1¼ cups double (heavy) or whipping cream
200g/7oz savoiardi or sponge finger biscuits (cookies)
90g/3½oz/generous ½ cup almonds, finely chopped and toasted
geranium flowers and icing (confectioners') sugar, to decorate

1 Put the sugar and water in a heavy pan and heat gently, stirring occasionally, until the sugar has dissolved completely.

2 Add the rose geranium leaves to the pan and cook gently for 2 minutes. Leave to cool.

COOK'S TIP

If you cannot get savoiardi biscuits, use ordinary sponge finger biscuits instead. These tend to be smaller, though, so you will need to adjust the size of the rectangle accordingly.

3 Strain the cooled geranium syrup into a measuring jug (pitcher) and then stir in the lemon juice.

4 Put the mascarpone in a bowl and beat it until it has softened. Gradually beat in 150ml/¼ pint/⅔ cup of the syrup mixture.

5 Whip the cream until it forms peaks, then fold it into the mascarpone and syrup mixture. At this stage the mixture should hold its shape. If necessary, whip the mixture a little more.

6 Spoon a little of the mixture on to a flat, freezerproof serving plate and spread it out with a palette knife (metal spatula) to a 21 × 12cm/8½ × 4½in rectangle.

7 Pour the remaining geranium syrup into a shallow bowl. Dip a savoiardi or sponge finger biscuit into the syrup until it is moist but not disintegrating. Place on to the rectangle. Repeat with a third of the biscuits to cover the rectangle completely.

8 Spread another thin layer of the cream mixture over the biscuits. Set aside 15ml/1 tbsp of the nuts for the topping. Scatter half the remainder over the cream.

9 Make another two layers of the syrup-steeped biscuits, sandwiching them with more of the cream mixture and the remaining nuts, but leaving enough cream mixture to coat the dessert completely.

10 Spread the remaining cream mixture over the top and sides of the cake until it is evenly coated. Sprinkle with the reserved nuts. Freeze it for at least 5 hours or overnight.

11 Transfer the marquise to the refrigerator for 30 minutes before serving, so that it softens slightly. Scatter with geranium flowers, dust with icing sugar, and serve in slices.

VARIATION

If you prefer, use other kinds of nuts instead of the almonds used here. Macadamia nuts and walnuts would both work well.

LYCHEE AND ELDERFLOWER SORBET

THE MUSCAT FLAVOUR OF ELDERFLOWERS IS WONDERFUL WITH SCENTED LYCHEES. SERVE THIS SOPHISTICATED SORBET AFTER A RICH MAIN COURSE.

SERVES FOUR

INGREDIENTS

175g/6oz/scant 1 cup caster
   (superfine) sugar
400ml/14fl oz/1⅔ cups water
500g/1¼lb fresh lychees, peeled
   and pitted
15ml/1 tbsp elderflower cordial
dessert biscuits (cookies), to serve

COOK'S TIPS
• Switch the freezer to the coldest setting before making the sorbet – the faster the mixture freezes, the smaller the ice crystals and the better the texture.
• Use a metal freezerproof container for best results.

1 Place the sugar and water in a pan and heat gently until the sugar has dissolved. Increase the heat and boil for 5 minutes, then add the lychees. Lower the heat and simmer for 7 minutes. Remove from the heat and allow to cool.

2 Purée the fruit and syrup in a food processor or blender, then press as much as you can through a sieve into a bowl.

3 By hand: Stir the elderflower cordial into the purée (paste), pour into a freezerproof container. Freeze for 2 hours, or until crystals form around the edge. Process briefly in a food processor or blender to break up the crystals. Repeat twice, then freeze until firm.
Using an ice cream maker: Pour the elderflower cordial and the purée into an ice cream maker. Churn until the sorbet is firm enough to scoop.

4 Transfer to the refrigerator for 10 minutes to soften. Serve with biscuits.

COCONUT AND LEMON GRASS ICE CREAM WITH LIME SYRUP

LEMON GRASS, A VERSATILE FLAVOURING WHICH IS WIDELY USED IN ASIAN COOKERY, MELDS WITH LIME TO ADD AN EXOTIC FRAGRANCE TO ICE CREAM. IF YOU CANNOT GET FRESH LEMON GRASS STALKS, USE THE DRIED STALKS THAT COME IN JARS.

SERVES FIVE TO SIX

INGREDIENTS

   4 lemon grass stalks
   400ml/14fl oz/1⅔ cups coconut milk
   3 egg yolks
   90g/3½oz/½ cup caster (superfine)
    sugar
   10ml/2 tsp cornflour (cornstarch)
   150ml/¼ pint/⅔ cup whipping cream
   finely grated (shredded) rind of 1 lime
   lime slices, to decorate
For the lime syrup
   75g/3oz/6 tbsp caster (superfine)
    sugar
   75ml/5 tbsp water
   1 lime, very thinly sliced, plus
    30ml/2 tbsp lime juice

1 Cut the lemon grass stalks in half lengthways and bruise the stalks by tapping them with a rolling pin. Put them in a heavy pan, add the coconut milk and bring to just below boiling point. Remove from the heat and leave to infuse (steep) for 30 minutes, then remove the lemon grass.

2 Whisk the egg yolks in a bowl with the sugar and cornflour until smooth. Gradually pour the coconut and lemon grass milk over the mixture, whisking well. Return the mixture to the pan and heat very gently, stirring until the custard starts to thicken. Do not let it boil or it may curdle.

3 Remove the custard from the heat and strain it into a clean bowl. Cover with a circle of dampened greaseproof (waxed) paper to prevent a skin forming. Leave to cool.

4 By hand: Whip the cream until it has thickened but still falls from the whisk, and stir into the custard with the lime rind. Transfer the mixture to a freezerproof container and freeze for 2 hours. Remove from the freezer and beat using a fork, a whisk or a food processor to break up the ice crystals. Freeze for another 2 hours then beat the mixture again.
Using an ice cream maker: Stir the cream and lime rind into the cooled custard. Churn.

5 Spoon the mixture into five or six dariole moulds. Freeze for at least 3 hours.

6 Meanwhile, make the lime syrup. Heat the sugar and water in a small, heavy pan until the sugar dissolves. Bring to the boil and allow to boil for 5 minutes without stirring. Reduce the heat, add the thinly sliced lime and the lime juice and simmer the syrup gently for 5 minutes more. Leave to cool.

7 To serve, loosen the edges of the dariole moulds with a knife. Dip them in very hot water for 2 seconds then turn out the ice creams on to dessert plates. Serve with the lime syrup and the lime slices spooned around.

BAY AND RATAFIA SLICE

THE WARM BUT DELICATE FLAVOUR OF BAY LEAVES COMBINES PARTICULARLY WELL WITH ALMOND FLAVOURS. SERVE THIS SUMPTUOUS SLICE WITH FRESH APRICOTS, PLUMS, PEACHES OR SOFT FRUITS. AN EXCELLENT DINNER-PARTY DESSERT THAT CAN BE MADE IN ADVANCE.

SERVES SIX

INGREDIENTS
  300ml/½ pint/1¼ cups milk
  4 fresh bay leaves
  4 egg yolks
  75g/3oz/6 tbsp caster (superfine)
    sugar
  10ml/2 tsp cornflour (cornstarch)
  150g/5oz ratafia (almond macaroons)
    or macaroon biscuits (cookies)
  300ml/½ pint/1¼ cups whipping
    cream

1 Put the milk in a pan, add the bay leaves and bring slowly to the boil. Remove from the heat and infuse (steep) for 30 minutes. Meanwhile, whisk the egg yolks in a bowl with the sugar and cornflour.

2 Strain the milk over the egg yolk mixture and stir well. Return to the pan and cook over a gentle heat, stirring constantly until the custard thickens. Do not let it boil or it may curdle. Transfer the custard to a bowl, cover closely with greaseproof (waxed) paper and leave to cool completely. Chill until very cold.

3 Crush the biscuits in a strong plastic bag, using a rolling pin.

4 By hand: Whip the cream until it has thickened but still falls from the whisk, and stir into the custard. Transfer to a freezerproof container. Freeze for about 4 hours, beating twice using a fork, a hand whisk or a food processor to break up the ice crystals. Stir in 50g/2oz of the crushed biscuits and freeze for a further 2 hours.
Using an ice cream maker: Add the cream to the custard and churn until it is very thick. Scrape it into a bowl and add 50g/2oz of the crushed biscuits. Return to the ice cream maker and churn for 2 minutes more.

5 Working quickly, spoon the ice cream on to a sheet of greaseproof paper, packing it into a log shape, about 5cm/2in thick and 25cm/10in long.

6 Bring the greaseproof paper up around the ice cream to pack it together tightly and give it a good shape. Support on a baking sheet and freeze for at least 3 hours or overnight.

7 Spread the remaining crushed biscuits on a sheet of greaseproof paper. Unwrap the ice cream log and roll it quickly in the crumbs until coated. Return to the freezer until needed. Serve in slices.

COOK'S TIP
If the ice cream is not firm enough to roll, freeze for a couple of hours more.

GOOSEBERRY AND ELDERFLOWER SORBET

A CLASSIC COMBINATION THAT MAKES A REALLY REFRESHING SORBET. MAKE IT IN SUMMER, AS A STUNNING FINALE TO AN AL FRESCO MEAL, OR SAVE IT FOR SERVING AFTER A HEARTY WINTER STEW.

SERVES SIX

INGREDIENTS

150g/5oz/¾ cup caster (superfine)
   sugar
175ml/6fl oz/¾ cup water
10 elderflower heads
500g/1¼ lb/5 cups gooseberries
200ml/7fl oz/scant 1 cup apple juice
dash of green food colouring (optional)
a little beaten egg white and caster
   (superfine) sugar, to decorate
   the glasses
elderflowers, to decorate

1 Put 30ml/2 tbsp of the sugar in a pan with 30ml/2 tbsp of the water. Set aside. Mix the remaining sugar and water in a separate, heavy pan. Heat them gently, stirring occasionally, until dissolved. Bring to the boil and boil for 1 minute, without stirring, to make a syrup.

2 Remove from the heat and add the elderflower heads, pressing them into the syrup with a wooden spoon. Leave to infuse (steep) for about 1 hour.

3 Strain the elderflower syrup through a sieve placed over a bowl. Set the syrup aside. Add the gooseberries to the pan containing the reserved sugar and water. Cover and cook very gently for about 5 minutes until the gooseberries have softened and the juices have started to run.

COOK'S TIP
Elderflowers can only be picked for a very short time. At other times, use 90ml/6 tbsp elderflower cordial.

4 Tip the mixture into a food processor and add the apple juice. Process until smooth, then press the purée (paste) through a sieve into a bowl. Leave to cool. Stir in the elderflower syrup, with a dash of green food colouring, if you like. Chill until very cold.

5 By hand: Pour into a freezerproof container. Freeze for 2 hours, or until crystals start to form around the edges. Process briefly in a food processor or blender to break up the crystals. Repeat twice more, then freeze until firm.
Using an ice cream maker: Churn the mixture until it holds its shape. Scrape it into a freezer container and freeze for several hours or overnight, until firm.

6 To decorate the glasses, put a little egg white in a bowl. Spread out the caster sugar on a plate. Dip the rim of each glass in the egg white, then into the sugar. Allow to dry for a few minutes. Soften the sorbet in the refrigerator and serve, decorated with elderflowers.

INDEX

baked fennel with a crumb crust 81
baked herb crêpes 84
baked tuna with a coriander crust 53
basil 21
  halibut fillets with fresh tomato and basil salsa 49
  melon and basil soup 27
  risotto with basil and ricotta 68
  roasted tomato and mozzarella salad with basil dressing 32
  saffron and basil breadsticks 95
bay 20
  bay and ratafia slice 126
  roast monkfish with garlic and bay leaves 54
bell pepper 17
  fried peppers with cheese and parsley 80
  minted potato and red pepper frittata 82
  roasted pepper and onion soup 31
black pepper 22
borage 17
bresaola and rocket pizza 85

caraway 17
cardamom 19
  bananas with lime and cardamom sauce 111
  kulfi with cardamom 119
cassoulet de Languedoc 64
chervil 16
chicken with fresh herbs and garlic 58
chicken salad with herbs and lavender 40
chilli 17
chives 16
  potato and mussel salad with shallot and chive dressing 37
chorizo with garlic potatoes 65
cilantro see coriander
cinnamon 18
cod: pan-fried with creamy vermouth and herb sauce 50
coriander 18
  baked tuna with a coriander crust 53
  Thai vegetable and coriander curry with lemon grass jasmine rice 72
cucumber and garlic soup with walnuts 28
curry: Thai vegetable and coriander curry with lemon grass jasmine rice 72

dill 16
  cucumber and dill salad 34
  sorrel, spinach and dill soup 26
drying herbs 14–15

elderflower 23
  gooseberry and elderflower sorbet 127
  lychee and elderflower sorbet 124

fennel 19
  baked chicken with shallots, garlic and fennel 56
  baked fennel with a crumb crust 81

cauliflower and bean soup with fennel seed and parsley 30
fennel and egg tabbouleh with herbs 36
fennel, orange and rocket salad 35
tomato, fennel and parsley pizza 87
fillets of hake baked with thyme and garlic 52
freezing herbs 15
French tarragon see tarragon
fresh herb risotto 70
fried peppers with cheese and parsley 80

garden flower pavlova 114
garlic 16
  baked chicken with shallots, garlic and fennel 56
  chicken with fresh herbs and garlic 58
  chorizo with garlic potatoes 65
  cucumber and garlic soup with walnuts 28
  roast garlic with goat's cheese, walnut and herb pâté 42
  roast monkfish with garlic and bay leaves 54
grilled cod fillet with fresh mixed herb crust 46
grilled red mullet with rosemary 47
ginger 23
growing herbs 8–13

harvesting herbs 14
herb gardens 8-13
horseradish 16

lavender 20
  chicken salad with herbs and lavender 40
  lavender and thyme chicken 57
  lavender cake 101
  lavender heart cookies 102
  lavender scones 100
  strawberry and lavender sorbet 118
lemon 18
  lamb steaks with mint and lemon 63
  lemon and herb risotto cake 71
  lemon and walnut cake 103
  little onions with coriander, wine and olive oil 41
lemon balm 20
lemon grass 18
  coconut and lemon grass ice cream with lime syrup 125
  lemon grass pork chops with mushrooms 61
  lemon grass skewers with lime cheese 116
  rabbit and lemon grass risotto 62
  Thai vegetable and coriander curry with lemon grass jasmine rice 72
little onions with coriander, wine and olive oil 41
lovage 20

marjoram 21
  chicken salad with herbs and lavender 40
mint: fennel and egg tabbouleh with herbs 36

lamb steaks with mint and lemon 63
mint ice cream 117
minted potato and red pepper frittata 82
mixed herb salad with toasted sunflower and pumpkin seeds 32
mustard 17

nasturtium 23
nutmeg 20

olive 21
  olive and oregano bread 96
  vegetables with tapenade and herb aioli 43
onion 16
  little onions with coriander, wine and olive oil 41
  red onion and goat's cheese pastries 78
  roasted pepper and onion soup 31
  sherried onion and saffron soup with almonds 29
opium poppy see poppy
oregano 21
  olive and oregano bread 96

pan-fried cod with creamy vermouth and herb sauce 50
pansotti with herbs and cheese 74
parsley 22
  cauliflower and bean soup with fennel seed and parsley 30
  fried peppers with cheese and parsley 80
  salad of fresh ceps with parsley and walnut dressing 38
  tomato, fennel and parsley pizza 87
pepper see bell pepper; black pepper
poppy 21
  poppy-seeded bloomer 92
potato and mussel salad with shallot and chive dressing 37

rabbit and lemon grass risotto 62
rocket 19
  bresaola and rocket pizza 85
  fennel, orange and rocket salad 35
  rocket and tomato pizza 86
red onion and goat's cheese pastries 78
roast monkfish with garlic and bay leaves 54
rocket and tomato pizza 86
rose 22
  apple and rose-petal snow 110
  raspberry and rose-petal shortcakes 108
  rosepetal sorbet decorated with sugared rose petals 121
rose geranium marquise 122
rosemary 22

grilled red mullet with rosemary 47
Italian flat bread with rosemary 90
rosemary ice cream 120
rosemary risotto with borlotti beans 69

saffron focaccia with rosemary topping 91

saffron 18
  saffron and basil breadsticks 95
  saffron focaccia with rosemary topping 91
  sherried onion and saffron soup with almonds 29
sage 22
salad burnet 23
sorrel 22
  sorrel, spinach and dill soup 26
storing herbs 15
strawberry 19
  strawberry and lavender sorbet 118
summer herb ricotta flan 78
summer savory 23
sunflower 23
  mixed herb salad with toasted sunflower and pumpkin seeds 32
  sunflower sultana scones 104
sweet cicely 21
sweet marjoram see marjoram

tagliatelli with herbs 76
tarragon 17
  chicken with tarragon cream 59
  panfried salmon with tarragon and mushroom sauce 51
Thai vegetable and coriander curry with lemon grass jasmine rice 72
thyme 23
  fillets of hake baked with thyme and garlic 52
  frittata with tomatoes and thyme 83
  lavender and thyme chicken 57
tomato, fennel and parsley pizza 87
treacle, date with walnut cake 105
turmeric 18

vegetables with tapenade and herb aioli 43
vermicelli with herb frittata 77

walnut 20
  cucumber and garlic soup with walnuts 28
  lemon and walnut cake 103
  and walnut meringue gâteau 115
  pain aux noix 99
  roast garlic with goat's cheese, walnut and herb pâté 42
  salad of fresh ceps with parsley and walnut dressing 38
  treacle, date with walnut cake 105
  walnut shortbread with spiced apple slices 112
warm herby bread 94
Welsh clay-pot loaves with herbs 98